D0121019

Rural Schools in Angus

RURAL
SCHOOLS
in
ANGUS

Dorothy Morrison

and

Isobel Reynolds

The Pinkfoot Press
Balgavies, Angus
2004

Published 2004 in Scotland by
The Pinkfoot Press
Balgavies, Forfar, Angus DD8 2TH
in collaboration with
Angus Council, Cultural Services

ISBN 1 874012 44 X

Typeset and designed at The Pinkfoot Press
Printed by The Cromwell Press, Trowbridge

Contents

Illustrations

Acknowledgements

As well as those who have contributed their memories of their schooldays in Angus we would like to thank the following people who have given us information, practical help, and in some cases access to their property. Their kindness has been much appreciated.

Norman Atkinson; Diana Bowen-Jones; The Rev Graham Bruce; Catherine Christieson; Margaret Colville; Dorothy and Ian Cruickshank; Rev Iain and Mrs Douglas; Mrs Drummond, Letham; Janette Fairlie; Anne Gibb; Ishbel Kydd; Michael and Hilary Laver; Neil Lawson; Michael Maltman; Norman Mill; Myra and Ian Millar; Ruth Millar; David and Kathleen Page; Nigel and Sheila Ruckley; Christine Saark; Claire Savage; David and Sarah Sayers; Jean Stevenson; Anthony and Magdalene Ward

Particular thanks is due to Angela Mathers of the 'Craigie Column' of *The Courier*, and to Innes Morrison who scanned all the illustrations

Illustrations

The authors are grateful to those people who have granted permission to reproduce illustrations:

Rosina McNicoll, head teacher, Newtyle PS (**1, 71**); David and Kathleen Page (**31, 38c**); Michael and Hilary Laver (**33**); Ian and Dorothy Cruikshank (**38b**); Evelyn Luke (**40**); Alison Stedman (**41–3**); William Thomson (**45**); Tayside Postcard Club (**46**); Bill Beedie (**47–8**); Mrs Cooper (**49**); Jim Mearns (**50**); Pam Cranswick (**55–6**); Agnes Riddell (**58–9**); Evelyn Mouat (**60**); Margaret Budge (**62**); Winnie MacDonald (**63**); Celia Gray (**64**); *The Courier* (**66–9, 72–4, 76**); Kimprint, Forfar (**78**)

All other illustrations are the property of the authors.

Introduction

The closure of a rural primary school usually causes great distress not only to the parents and children affected but to the whole community of which it forms a part. A village primary school can provide a focus for much neighbourhood activity and foster a strong sense of local identity. In spite of the material advantages and opportunities which the larger, more modern school may provide, for many parents these are outweighed by the very real benefits their children may experience in the smaller, community friendly school close to home.

There is a great deal of sympathy for this point of view especially among older people who themselves enjoyed a village education but the circumstances which created the scattered rural schools of Angus have changed drastically over the last forty years. Increasingly there is no longer a viable school population in many areas as the number of people involved in agriculture has steadily decreased. Many of the older school buildings now require major financial outlay to enable them to reach modern requirements. All too often the solution has been to close the smaller schools. In many cases this has coincided with the demise of the village shop and Post Office. In rural areas nowadays the local church often forms part of a linked charge serving several parishes. In these circumstances a school closure can strike a death blow to community activities. The strenuous efforts of local groups to avoid losing their school are fully understandable. Happily a number of rural schools have been modernised and extended in recent years to a very high standard and at least one fine new rural school has been opened.

All over Angus the evidence of a vanished way of life can be seen in the number and variety of former schools and schoolhouses which have now taken on a different role. The sound construction of many nineteenth century buildings has made them ideally suited to conversion into distinctive and attractive modern homes. We have taken great delight in seeing the varied solutions the new owners have found. In some cases the former schools still cater for the public as craft centres, tea rooms or workshops. Angus College has taken over one school building as overspill accommodation. For the most part the conversions are sympathetic to the original structure of the buildings and we can only regret the few instances where once thriving schools have been reduced to mere storage sheds.

The rural schools of Angus have a history which deserves to be celebrated. The schoolmasters and schoolmistresses who spent long years coping with large classes of varying ages and ability faced many problems. Yet many of their pupils went on to achieve great things and all received a sound, basic education. We have called on many different sources to tell their fascinating story and are particularly grateful to those former pupils and teachers who shared their memories and mementoes with us.

1 *Newtyle pupils at Ancrum Road Victorian classroom*

2 *The simple school building built in 1814 in the village of St.Vigeans*

The Historical Background

Before 1872

When compulsory education was introduced into Scotland in 1872, a great school building programme began. Many of the converted school buildings in rural Angus date from that time but a number of older schools can still be traced. In some parts of the county school provision was good enough for the earlier school buildings to remain in use for some years.

Scotland had long prided itself on its educational provisions and sixteenth-century standards were high in the teaching of 'gentle and honest mens berns of the cowntrey' round about Angus. James Melvill, born in 1557, had fond memories of his schooldays

> *About the fyft yeir of my age, the Grate Buik was put in my hand, and when I was seavine, lytle thereof haid I lernit at hame; therefor my father put my eldest and onlie brother David, about a yeir and a halff in age aboue me, and me togidder to a kinsman and brother in the ministerie of his to scholl, a guid, lerned, kynd man, whome for thankfulness I name, Mr. Wilyam Gray, minister of Logie, Montrose. He haid a sister, a godlie and honest matron, rewler of his hous, wha often rememberit me of my mother, and was a verie lowing mother to ws indeid. Ther was a guid nomber of gentle and honest mens berns of the cowntrey about, weill treaned bathe in letters, godlinesse and exercise in honest geams. Ther we lerned to reid the Catechisme, prayers and scripture, to rehers the catechisme and prayers par ceur, also nottes of Scripture efter the reiding thereof ... We lerned there the Rudiments of the Latin grammair, with the vocables in Latin and Frenche, also divers speithches in Frenche, with the reiding and right pronunciation of that toung. We proceidit fordar to the Etymologie of Lilius, and his Syntax, as also a lytle of the Syntax of Linacer; ... He had a verie guid and profitable form of resoluing the authors, he teached grammaticallie bathe according to the Etymologie and syntax; bot as for me, the trewthe was, my imgyne and memorie war guid aneuche, bot my judgment and understanding was as yit smored and dark, sa that the thing quilk I gat was mair be rat ryme nor knawlege.*
>
> *Ther also we haid the aire guid, and fields reasonable near; and be our maister war teached to handle the bow for archerie, the glub for goff, the batons for fencing; also to rin, to loope, to swoum, to warsell, to proue pratteiks, everie ane haiffing his matche and andagonist, bathe in our lessons and play. A happie and golden tyme indeid.*

Certainly as far as legal requirements went there were grounds for satisfaction. As far back as 1616 the Privy Council had issued an Act for establishing schools in every parish. In 1650 five schools were established in the Presbytery of Brechin – Maryton, Farnell, Menmuir, Dun, and Logie Pert. Arbirlot benefited in 1692 when Sir Alexander Irvine left an endowment of £7 annually towards the salary of the parish teacher.

An Education act of 1696 had made it compulsory for the heritors of each parish to set up or maintain a school but since these landowners were reluctant for the most part to pay the tax on the annual value of their land which would fund this provision, it was largely ineffective. Only 10 parishes in Angus had a school in the seventeenth century.

The Jacobite rising of 1715 had an impact for some time on education in Angus for both the Earls of Panmure and Southesk supported the Jacobite cause and their estates were forfeit as a result. A considerable number of teachers were Jacobite supporters and were later removed from their posts by the Presbytery and local Kirk Sessions. John Cofts was deposed from Fern and David Walker from Farnell.

The *Old Statistical Account* of the early 1790s reveals some of the successes as well as the inadequacies in school provision in Angus. The Rev Thomas Wright, describing the parish of Rescobie happily stated that 'intellectual improvement proceeds apace'. Whereas in 1777 there were three very elderly people who could not read, by 1793 there were none. 'Children are sent early in life to school' he claimed. While every rural parish in Angus had a school by this time, it was not always conveniently located and was never adequately financed. Schoolmasters, in a time of increasing inflation, subsisted on miserably poor salaries. Thus at Menmuir the minister recorded:

> The encouragement given to the master is extremely poor. A paltry house, about 100 merks of salary, and the emoluments not about £2.

Most schoolmasters relied on supplementing their income by acting as session clerk and precentor to the parish church. Although not all were possessed of good singing voices they were usually required to officiate prior to appointment. Some must have avoided a public display for the minister at Fern in 1779 complained that the schoolmaster's singing of the psalms 'was like to wear out of the church'.

A fee for recording baptisms and marriages might add a little more, although some parishioners neglected to have these important occasions recorded. More fortunate schoolmasters might also have a house, a garden and a small glebe. At Tealing the 'badness of the road in the winter season' discouraged scholars while at Liff and Benvie it was noted

> the situation is centrical enough with respect to the whole district, but yet not very commodious for one or two places, which contain by far, the greater number of the inhabitants. Besides, the access to school from the west, is in great measure shut up, and in winter the roads in every other direction are to children almost impassable.

Not surprisingly the school was in 'a low state' and the 'whole emoluments too inconsiderable for a teacher of any merit and capacity'.

Prior to 1872 the church had a strong hold over education provision and for the most part the church schools provided a fairly good education. This extract from the Kirk Session records of Montrose shows what was expected of a school and schoolmaster in 1811. Some complaints had been received from parents of scholars at the Sessional School at Loanhead (Hillside) who claimed that the teacher, Donald Fleming,

> *having been brought up in the Highlands ... is altogether unqualified for instructing children in the proper sounds and pronunciation of the English Language.*

Furthermore they alleged

> *His abilities in Arithmetic were so slender that although after his admission he commenced an evening school for boys and those of more advanced years the whole of them left before the expiry of the first quarter, and he has had none since.*

The Presbytery decided to act and the poor teacher, whose annual salary was £2 and a free house, received a visit from a delegation of four ministers. They conducted an examination not only of the scholars but of Fleming himself. He had prudently ensured that the pupils were well versed in the Psalms and Catechism and the report which followed was very favourable stating,

> *That they had examined Donald Fleming on English, Reading, Spelling, Writing, on the principles of Religion, in Arithmetic, as far as the Rule of Proportion, & vulgar fractions, on all which he gave them entire satisfaction, & particularly in his expertness in the above branches of Arithmetic.*

In what might be described as the Highland areas of Angus the SPCK (Society for Propagating Christian Knowledge) set up schools in parts of parishes without any. There were SPCK schools at the Bridge of Tarf, Glen Esk, Kilry, Glen Isla, and in Glen Clova. All SPCK teachers had to undergo an examination by a committee in Edinburgh in reading, writing, arithmetic and religion. Small private or Adventure schools often operated although these were not encouraged by church authorities as being 'a great Discouragement to the schoolmaster' since he relied on the pupils' fees for part of his income.

From 1833 the Government gave grants to voluntary societies to run schools and by 1840 appointed inspectors to see that the money was properly spent. The pupil-teacher system was introduced in 1846. This paid boys or girls to stay on at school both teaching and studying. If they passed the necessary examination each year by the inspector they could go by the age of 17, either to Edinburgh or Glasgow for further teacher training at the 'normal colleges' which had been founded in the 1830s.

However, prior to 1872 the only national system of education in Scotland was that provided by the parish schools and this was often far from ideal. In Guthrie parish, until 1872, schoolchildren attended a school at the Cotton of Guthrie in an old cottar house. Here one dominie presided over up to 100 children.

The Disruption of the Church of Scotland in 1843 had a major influence on education in Scotland for many schoolmasters elected to join the Free Church. In many cases, as in Craig, Carmyllie and Lochlee in Angus they were compelled to give up their schools. The Free Church made valiant efforts to establish its own schools and 'normal' schools. In Hillside a Free Church school for girls operated briefly from 1856 to 1860. In several places in Angus however, Lord Panmure, a chief heritor in many parishes, refused sites for Free Church schools. His son and heir, later Lord Dalhousie, took a different view and in fact subscribed to their erection.

3 *Montrose from Craig*

While the parish school system, supplemented by the establishment of Free Church schools, operated fairly well in rural areas such as Angus, it was completely inadequate by the mid 19th century for a developing industrialised society. The speedy growth of population in the larger towns and cities helped to break down the old parochial system. The aim of the 1872 (Scotland) Act was that 'efficient education for their children may be furnished and made available to the whole people of Scotland'. It was now the duty of every parent to provide elementary education in reading, writing and arithmetic for his children between 5 and 13 years of age.

The Act set up the Scotch Education Department as a central authority and provided School Boards elected by ratepayers to administer schools. Church control came to an end although Kirk Sessions did nominate representatives to the school boards. The Church of Scotland and the Free Church gave over their schools unconditionally. It was thus possible for the 1872 Act to come into effect immediately while the new Board Schools were being built. In England the equivalent 1870 Act was phased in over a ten-year period.

Parish Schoolmasters

The status of the dominie

The early parish schoolmasters were poorly paid and poorly housed but by the 18th century the rural schoolmaster, or dominie, together with the minister, held a position of considerable respect and status in the community and many highly qualified men were eager to obtain a position which offered standing and influence. By the act of 1696, the office of schoolmaster had a degree of official recognition enjoyed by few other occupations. Schoolmasters were entitled to a house, a small garden and a basic income which could be added to by payment for other duties such as those of precentor and session clerk. While the schoolmaster was under the supervision of the minister and the local heritors, he did have some security of tenure. It was not easy to dismiss a parochial schoolmaster for he held his office under the law and substantiating complaints against him was a lengthy procedure involving official Presbytery hearings. Before the passing of the Parochial and Burgh Schoolmasters (Scotland) Act in 1861 dominies, although incompetent or infirm, could not be required to resign. At Loanhead (Hillside) in 1811, when Donald Fleming was dismissed from his post on the grounds that he was unqualified to teach, he took his case to the Sheriff Court which found in his favour and ordered the Session to reinstate him and pay his legal expenses and outstanding salary. At Maryton in 1830 when the minister lodged a complaint against the dominie for drunkenness, cruel and improper treatment of the scholars and a neglect of his duty, the schoolmaster appeared before the Presbytery and two heritors of the parish accompanied by his counsel. The hearing went on well into the evening and the evidence given in justification of his subsequent dismissal was not entered in the Presbytery records.

The Church and education

The close connection between the church and education in Scotland make Kirk Session and Presbytery records a main source of information regarding schools and schoolmasters. The troubled politics and religious controversies of the 17th century made it difficult to achieve the ideal of a school in every parish but in 1650 the Presbytery of Brechin, influenced by the strong Directions delivered by the General Assembly the previous year, took the first steps to 'settle scholes with ane competent provision and ane qualified schoolmaster in every congregation'. The late 1640s and 1650s were difficult times in Angus as plagues, Civil War and Cromwell's troops all added to the miseries of the countryside. It was some years before adequate maintenance from the heritors made it possible to appoint and keep schoolmasters in many parishes.

In 1656 we find that a school met in the Kirk of Inchbrayock under a schoolmaster of good behaviour who 'was approven for his sober conversation'. The schoolmaster appointed at Farnell the following year, Mr David Carnegy, was 'approven be the minister and elders in his Christian lyke carriage and diligence'. The schoolmaster at Inchbrayock, or his successor however ran into trouble some years later for, in 1667, he was summoned before the Presbytery for employing 'unlawful art for recovering of stollen goods'. He appears to have tried to divine the whereabouts of the goods by magic. His curious explanation that he only 'rolled some stones' earned him a sharp rebuke but he remained in office. Six years later, having moved to the school at Logy, he was again summoned before the Presbytery. He had married a younger daughter of the Earl of Southesk in questionable circumstances 'without any order or consent of parents or proclamationes'. Only by appearing humbly on three successive Sundays before the whole congregation of Logy was he able to remain in his post.

4 The much-altered original 300-year-old Logie schoolhouse was a wattle and daub construction made of dried clay bound with pebbles and straw. The roof would have been thatched. Logie children attended this school until 1929 when Craigo school opened. When the Den Kirk returned to the Church of Scotland, the empty Logie School was given to the United Free congregation by Mr MacPherson Grant to Mr Dutch, a church member, local agent for Biblical books and local attendance officer

Problems for schoolmasters

Throughout the 18th century, schoolmasters were, in general, very poorly paid. In 1748 and again in 1782 they framed a memorial to be presented to the General Assembly and to Parliament asking that their salaries might be increased. This had no success since ministers, though sympathetic, were also seeking an increase in their own stipends.

The Kirk Session records of the early 18th century reveal the continuing problems any aspiring schoolmaster faced in Angus. The case of poor David Aitken, schoolmaster and precentor at Stracathro, was not unusual. He had no schoolhouse and only a payment of eleven firlots of meal and other occasional offerings. With few scholars, and those attending only in wintertime, he could add little to his income through fees. There was no provision for a dominie suffering illness or becoming too old to work unless he chose to retain his post. In 1713 the former master of the school in the kirk at Maryton who had lost his sight 'by reason of age' and was no longer able to teach, appealed to the Presbytery for help. Lacking money, they could only commend him to the goodwill of 'all Charitable Christians'. Another unfortunate, James Bruce, schoolmaster at Fern for over twenty years, had a bad fall from a house in 1743. He 'was so bruised as to bring on him a Paralitick Distemper' so that he could neither teach nor carry our the duties of Session Clerk and precentor. The tenants who normally would be required to contribute to his salary refused to offer him more than 'oats when he should apply for them in Time of Oatsecd' although a verbal agreement had been made at the time of his resignation that he would be given at least part of his stipend. Poor man! He would have been better to refuse to resign as did the schoolmaster at Eassie and Nevay. He gave up teaching in 1841 due to ill-health but still kept his full salary. The assistant who did all the teaching in the school had the schoolmaster's house and garden and the school fees. Similarly the parish schoolmaster at Monifieth in 1842 did not have the full salary as the heritors paid £48 yearly to the old schoolmaster 'who had become unfitted for his laborious duties'.

A more settled society

The political upsets consequent on the Jacobite risings, which had much support in Angus, caused further difficulties for schoolmasters. The schoolmaster at Fern, John Crofts, was one of the many removed after 1716 because of Jacobite leanings. As the 18th century progressed, a more settled society greatly encouraged the development of the parochial school system. At Maryton the building of a new school in 1726 enabled the Session to seek a well-qualified dominie and after a while Mr Hugh Chrystie, later principal teacher at the Grammar School in Montrose, was appointed. He published a Latin grammar which was widely used. His successor was obviously well-satisfied with his post for he remained as schoolmaster and Session Clerk at Maryton for the next sixty years.

Alexander Ross and other teacher 'poets'

Another example of long service was that of Alexander Ross who became schoolmaster at Lochlee, Glenesk in 1732. Initially the Brechin Presbytery was hesitant to confirm his appointment since his wife, Jean Cattenach, had 'been educated in the Popish religion'. When requested to produce his marriage certificate, the new schoolmaster admitted 'that he had none at present'. Such problems seem to have been overcome for Mr Ross remained at Lochlee for the next 50 years raising a large family in the small house and school beside the loch on a salary of little more than £20 a year. Like many parish schoolmasters Ross had a university education having graduated from Marischal College, but it was not until he reached the age of 70 that he published the Scots songs and poetry which had been his pastime over many years. By this time 'a good-humoured, social, happy old man', he was doubtless delighted by the immediate success of *Helenore, or, The Fortunate Shepherdess*. Burns referred to him as 'our true brother, Ross of Lochlee'. In the new churchyard of Lochlee the epitaph on his tombstone reads:

ERECTED

TO THE MEMORY

OF

ALEXANDER ROSS, AM.,

SCHOOLMASTER OF LOCHLEE

AUTHOR OF "LUNDY AND NORY; OR,

THE FORTUNATE SHEPHERDESS,"

AND OTHER POEMS IN SCOTTISH DIALECT.

BORN, APRIL, 1699

DIED, MAY 1784.

HOW FINELY NATURE AYE HE PAINTIT

O' SENSE IN RHYME HE NE'ER WAS STINTIT,

AN' TO THE HEART HE ALWAYS SENT IT

WI' MIGHT AND MAIN:

AN NO AE LINE HE E'ER INVENTIT

NEED ANE OFFEN'!

Mr Ross's predecessor at Lochlee had not distinguished himself as a schoolmaster. He was suspended by the Presbytery for a short period in 1723 having 'confessed drunkenness'. It would appear his problem persisted. Five years later, charged with breaking the Sabbath, he explained that 'through a gross Mistake of Memory, he had mistaken the Sabbath for Thursday'! On this occasion he lost his post.

Several Angus schoolmasters seem to have written poetry of one kind or another, although without the acclaim received by Alexander Ross. The schoolmaster at Glamis in 1729 published *The Assembly's Shorter Catechism in Metre for the use of young ones*. Whether 'young ones' found it any easier to learn than the normal compulsory catechism is doubtful as these two quotations show:

Question 1: **What is the chief end of man?**
The chief and highest end of man
is God to glorify,
keep his commandment, and enjoy
Him to eternity.

Question 2: **What rule hath God given?**
The only Rule infallible
Giv'n us for that intent,
Is God's good word, contained in
Th'Old and New Testament.

Similarly inspired to rhyme was Andrew Thomson of Kinnell who taught at Inverkeilor. In 1841 he published *Scotland a rhyming Geography in 32 pages*. The section on 'Angus or Forfar' concludes with the inspiring lines

Close by Southesk, on an incline,
And eight miles from the shore,
Lies Brechin, with two Tenaments,
The Upper and the Lower!

A more gifted writer in the Scots tongue perhaps was George Donald who was appointed to Tarfside School, Lochlee in 1847 and later to Forfar and St Vigeans. He did not have the educational advantages of Alexander Ross whose work he much admired. He started his working life as a 'herd laddie' and then a weaver but, largely self-taught, he was an early student at the new Normal School for the Training of Teachers. His work was very popular for many years not only in Scotland but also in Canada and America and no fewer than five editions of his poems were published. This extract from 'Mang oor ain folk at hame' gives a flavour of his writing.

Tho' nae star thro' the welkin in brightness appear.
The bright lamp o' friendship will lighten us here,
And fondly we'll pledge the dear friends o' the past,
Tho' mountains and billows between us are cast;
Their mem'ry, their worth, we'll aye cherish the same,
And they'll ever be dear to our ain folk at hame.

Another rural headmaster with a keen interest in writing and poetry was Mr Alex Taylor. He spent thirteen years as dominie at Guthrie and Newbigging and almost twenty years as headmaster at Kinloch and Carlogie Schools in Carnoustie, retiring at the end of 1984. He contributed articles and poetry to the *Scots Magazine* for many years, and in 1989 published a collection of articles and poems entitled *Angus Lore and Legend*. He too chose to write in Scots as this sample shows:

THE DEIL'S HALF-ACRE

A sad time this the early spring,
This sunshine disna gar me sing.
The daffodils, the snowdrops white,
Tae me present a fearfu' sight.
The birdies chirpin' in my lug,
Are whistling "Get that garden dug!"

The safter winds, the longer day,
They dinna join to mak' me gay,
The burstin' buds in ilka tree,
The lambs, they bring nae joy tae me,
For I have got a plot o' land,
A country gairden oot o' hand.

Cockfight Dues

One important source of income for the schoolmaster in the 18th century was the barbarous practice of cockfighting as an annual event in the school year. Game cocks were raised and trained by the scholars and brought to the school on Handsel Monday. The schoolroom became an arena and the cocks were set on each other fighting until one was disabled or killed. The schoolmaster got the dead birds and the boy whose cock survived victorious won a prize. By the early 19th century this practice was frowned upon in many places. At Tannadice, when a new schoolmaster was appointed in 1824, the heritors stated 'No cock-fighting to be permitted in the schoolroom, under any pretence, under the penalty of £2 to the poor of the parish, to be prosecuted for by the Kirk treasurer'. However the following year the schoolmaster at Tarfside, Lochlee was criticised in the *Montrose Review* for supervising an event lasting five hours at which 35 cocks took part. An irate correspondent wrote:

The practice of exhibiting cock fights annually at schools has, time-out-of-mind, use and wont in its favour, and every sentiment of feeling, humanity and religion against it. That a man who calls himself a schoolmaster and whose duty it is to inculcate the principles of Christianity and morality to his pupils, can easily stand beside his youthful charge, and superintend a scene of blood and butchery, is to us astonishing in the extreme.

The 1872 Act – More teachers

One result of the establishment of compulsory education was that many more teachers were needed to cope with the great influx of pupils so that salaries increased. There was no national rate of pay. Salaries were fixed by the appropriate School Board until 1918. Teachers could apply for an increase especially on securing extra qualifications, but this was often not successful.

In the early years of compulsory education some schools in Angus were hard-pressed to cope with the numbers of pupils enrolled. When the new school opened at Little Brechin on 10 November 1875 there were nine pupils on the roll. By 3 December the number of pupils had leapt to 57 and by 24 December there were 76 on the register. At Parkhouse School it was recorded in August 1879 that 'so many pupils entered that several had to be sent away. All rooms overcrowded'. At Inverkeilor School in the same year the limited space and the number of pupils crushed in to the old building made classroom organisation very difficult for the harassed teacher who wrote, 'organisation and discipline rendered very precarious from limited room and the atmosphere very impure'.

5 *A Kilry pupil in 2003 studying a 19th-century log book*

Log-books

With the introduction of compulsory education in 1872 the keeping of a log-book by the head teacher had become a requirement in every school. It would be looked at and signed by any visiting inspector to the school. The Scotch Code (See Appendix 2) stated that 'no reflections or opinions of a general nature are to be entered in the Log-Book'. Thus some Angus schoolmasters kept a faithful if dull record of the work carried out day by day in the school while noting any unusual events. Fortunately others, from time to time, used the log-book as a means of drawing attention to problems or inadequacies and perhaps of venting their feelings. One can sympathise with the country teacher in 1889 who records, 'am trying to get the boys of the Infants and Standard 1 to use the urinals instead of more exposed places'. The headmaster at Auchmithie found the atmosphere in the school in the summer months very difficult. In 1893 he complained about the noisome smell pervading the school and schoolhouse:

Atmosphere of the school very bad in consequence of a number of waggons containing manure. These waggons are often left for two days and when their contents are at last stirred up in such weather as we often have in June, the schoolrooms are almost uninhabitable. Unfortunately no redress can be obtained.

Ten years later he was still suffering from this problem and had at last complained to the School Board. An on-site inspection was made and the Board minuted in their report, 'a manure deposit is located in such close proximity to Auchmithie School as to be detrimental to the health of the scholars attending that school as well as of the teacher and his family'. Nothing further was done. A complaint to the School Board was often ineffectual as the schoolmaster at St Vigeans sadly pointed out in 1905 and again in the following year, 'pupils were being employed by the Earl of Northesk. The Earl was a member – albeit an absentee member – of the St. Vigeans School Board.'

The importance of headmasters in the community

The conscientious schoolmaster at Maryton over 20 years, Mr David Marr had greatly improved the standard of work in the school. (See page 55). He rarely made personal comments in the log-book but on 30 November 1894 he sadly recorded, 'not at all well and not so able for the work of the school as I would like to be'. He struggled on for a few more weeks before an interim teacher was appointed. On 12 April 1895 the log-book states, 'school closed on Monday because of Mr. Marr's funeral'. His obituary reveals the important place schoolmasters held in the community.

Mr David Marr

Died at Maryton Schoolhouse aged fifty-two. Twenty years ago he was appointed headmaster of Maryton Public School. Besides the ordinary school classes, Mr. Marr took a deep interest in the teaching of agriculture. He also held the offices of Registrar, Session Clerk, and Inspector of Poor of the parish of Maryton, and for a number of years he acted as Secretary to the Angus and Mearns Association of Inspectors of Poor. He was a fellow of the Educational Institute of Scotland.

Mr Robert Spalding

In a similar way headmaster Robert Spalding who died suddenly in September 1892 at the schoolhouse in Dun had served his local community for 29 years.

Himself an excellent scholar, he had the faculty of conveying his information to the pupils under him, several of whom have taken distinguished positions not only in commercial but in scholastic spheres. He also filled the offices of Inspector of Poor, Clerk to the School Board, and Clerk to the heritors in the parish of Dun, and in fact it might be said that in all matters affecting the parish he was the leading spirit, discharging his duties with efficiency and quietness.

When the respected headmaster of Kinnettles School retired in 1918 the official entry in the school log-book recorded,

he possessed the distinction of being the only old parochial teacher in this district and one of the few survivors of that body in Scotland. For over fifty years he has been actively engaged in the work of public instruction; to the end he has proved himself a competent and vigorous teacher who had always at heart the best interest of his pupils.

Sadness in the Schoolhouse

The log-books show that while classwork carried on in the schoolroom, there might be sad happenings in the adjacent schoolhouse. At Lunan the schoolmaster and his wife lost several of their children. It was expected that in spite of personal difficulties the headmaster and his family would not allow any interference with the running of the school or the fulfilling of the many other duties which were expected of them.

At Carroch in 1885 when the headmaster became ill on 23 January, a temporary teacher was employed, but Mr Burnett died ten days later. A brief note records that in March 'two children were withdrawn by removal of the late teacher's widow to Kirriemuir'. At Little Brechin in 1877 the log, written in the headmaster's hand, states that 'there has been no school today. Mrs. Morrison died at 10am yesterday aged 25'. At Padanaram in 1932 the teacher, Mr Doig, suffered a heart attack and his wife acted as interim teacher. It must have been difficult for Mrs Doig nursing a sick husband and running a school. Only nine months later her husband sadly records that 'Mrs Doig died this morning at 3.23am'.

6 *The gravestone in Lunan churchyard*

Salaries

Clearly such men wielded considerable influence locally and, on a salary of £150 per year and a schoolhouse, they could live comfortably. Since there was no national salary scale until 1918 however, the log-books reveal that some teachers were far from satisfied with their lot. Some School Boards were more generous than others. At Craig in 1894 the headmaster received £120 per annum plus his house, while at Ferryden the master's salary was £160, although his assistant received only £40. At Chapelton School in 1907 the headmaster, feeling at a low ebb, was moved to write indignantly,

I am debarred by medical certificate from attending school duties on account of acute dyspepsia caused by being unable on account of cost of living and no increase in salary to get half fed.

Perhaps his outburst made him feel better for the minute!

7 *Chapelton School has now become a family home*

Compensations

Some log-book entries reveal that the teacher's lot was sometimes rewarding. At Little Brechin 24 December 1879 brought a pleasant surprise.

This day my boys and girls had a surprise for me. I could not account for the restlessness of the school and to add to my wonder, my four biggest boys disappeared at 'Minutes'. I endeavoured in vain to discover why they had gone. All I learned was they had gone to Brechin. In the afternoon they appeared bringing with them a beautiful Christmas cake bearing the words 'presented to Mr and Mrs Mills by their pupils'. At the same time was presented a smaller cake to my little boy with suitable inscription. Mrs Mills was presented by the girls with a beautiful silver double jelly-glass as a token of their love and esteem.

In January 1926 the teacher at Rescobie wrote with some satisfaction, 'the school was closed on Thursday afternoon. There was an important curling match at [?]Culrash and the teacher was taking part in it'. He does not record the score!

School Inspections

The official HMI inspections were very important occasions for the headmaster. The first Government Inspectors' Report was published in 1842 but even before that headmasters were accustomed to regular visitations to the school by various local dignitaries particularly, in rural areas, the laird, his wife and the parish minister. Formal visitations often took place at the beginning of May and the end of October and these would entail a great deal of preparation for both master and pupils. The visits of the Government inspectors were particularly stressful since the inspectors, who often did not themselves have teaching experience, had the power to withhold the new Government grant if they considered the school in an unsatisfactory state. Under the Revised Scotch Code of 1862 an attempt was made to raise standards by introducing the idea of Payment by Results based on good attendance and proficiency in the subjects taught. This idea was emphasised further in 1872 so that the inspector's annual visit could decide just how much money was made available to a particular school for the coming year. Since the inspector's report was both submitted to the School Board and published in the local newspaper, the headmaster whose pupils failed to impress was in a difficult situation.

The Schools Code of 1874 (See Appendix 3) laid down very clearly what a Board school should teach. After the infant classes six standards were set for reading, writing and arithmetic with history and geography being added in standards 4, 5 and 6. As reading levels progressed there was an increasing emphasis on formal grammar.

Teachers desperate to do well on inspection day might therefore resort to a variety of tricks and dodges. Messages were passed from one school to another about the habits of particular inspectors. Various signs might be worked out between teacher and pupils. Non-readers were required to memorise passages. If at all possible teachers might try to avoid taking in likely failures, at least until after the inspector's visit. It is not surprising that even the best teachers would be forced to adopt rote learning, daily drill in reading and arithmetic and often a ready use of corporal punishment.

The Schoolmistress

The role of the woman teacher in Angus in the earlier years has not been so well-recorded, for the post of parish school teacher in the 17th and 18th centuries was invariably held by a man. The 16th-century diary of James Melvill makes mention of Miss Marjorie Gray, sister of the minister at Logie, 'a godlie and honest matron' who assisted her brother in his school there. On his marriage she established a 'hous and scholl for lasses' and this is perhaps an early mention of a 'Dame School'. In the next two centuries many ladies, widows or spinsters, chose to support themselves in this way, some by teaching the genteel domestic arts, some, as described by Sir John Sinclair, 'elderly women in the more humble walks of life', offering for a small fee a very basic introduction to reading and writing.

Such a teacher was Miss Jean Smart who taught at Inchbare round about 1825. The alphabet used at the school gives an insight into the abilities, background and pronunciation of both teacher and pupils.

> *Muckle   Ah*
> *Little   Ah*
> *Bey*
> *Say*
> *Day*
> *Fat's in yer heed?   E*
> *F*
> *Fat's like yer Mither's Glasses?   G*
> *H*
> *I*
> *J*
> *Fat's in the byre?   K*
> *Fat has ae leg?   L*
> *Fat has 3 legs?   M*
> *Fat has 2 legs?   N*
> *Fat's like the Mune?   O*
> *Pey*
> *Q*
> *Err*
> *Fat's like the crook?   S*
> *Fat's on yer feet?   Tae*
> *U*
> *Vey*
> *W*
> *Fat does yer Mither brak sticks wi'?   X*
> *Y*
> *Izzit*

A picture of how such an early 19th-century school might have looked is given by the Angus poet Alexander Smart in 'Madie's Schule'. He remembers his early education with affection when he would sit

> ' ... sae demure on a wee creepy stool
> And con owre my lesson in Auld Madie's schule.'

8 *Usan Village*

At the fishing village of Usan the long narrow schoolroom was presided over by just such a teacher known as 'The Missie'. Her two-apartment whitewashed house, perched on a high rock promontory, was surrounded by a grass plot where the school children played. One well-loved schoolmistress who later taught at Usan was Miss Margaret Gardyne. In 1830 she opened a school in Carmyllie seeking to teach both boys and girls the 3 Rs as well as dressmaking to the girls. She was so successful that by 1843 she had over 40 scholars. However she was forced to leave Carmyllie at the time of the Disruption in 1843 since both she and her widowed mother chose to support the Free Church. For the next 12 years she taught school at Kinnell where, in addition to the free house provided, she received a salary of £5 per annum and fees of 1d. per week from each pupil. Moving to Usan brought an increase in salary to £15 per annum plus fees and she stayed there, in her final post, for another nine years.

With the introduction of the pupil-teacher system in 1846, many girls of ability gained the necessary examination passes to enter the 'normal schools' in either Edinburgh or Glasgow, which had been set up in the 1830s, or the Free Church Colleges established after 1843. Here the emphasis was laid on the standard school subjects.

Not so many girls from rural areas went this far, although the small payments made to pupil-teachers did encourage some. It was much more likely that boys would proceed to further study. After all, girls were much more useful to their parents at home than in a classroom particularly if they were part of a large family. They could take part too in the seasonal work of the land especially at harvest time. The general belief was that domestic skills would be of the greatest use to a girl in her future life. Margaret Budge, herself a teacher, tells the story of a great aunt in a rural school who was told by a disgruntled parent, 'See you. You're that stuffed up wi' geography, ye'll never get a man!' It was with this attitude in mind that many parish schools offered sewing as part of the curriculum. Very often this was taught by the headmaster's wife. At Kinnell in October 1874 Mrs Gauldie, the wife of the new headmaster, was appointed as sewing teacher at £10 per year. In St Vigeans in 1876 where the wife of the headmaster also taught sewing, he recorded in his log-book, 'as the mistress got a son yesterday, I hardly expect her to appear at school the next fortnight or so'.

9 *The parents of St Vigeans fought an unsuccessful battle to keep the village school open*

When education became compulsory from the age of five in 1872 there was an immediate increase in the demand for teachers especially for children at the infant stage. The opportunities for women teachers were suddenly much greater and the new school boards were quick to appoint them as assistants. They were cheaper to employ even though as well qualified as many male headmasters. Women remained on a lower salary scale than men right up to 1960, when the argument that the breadwinner deserved a greater reward no longer seemed so obvious.

In November 1875 when the pupil teacher at Kinnell School left, a promising pupil, Ann Mann, was employed as monitor to teach some of the younger classes at a salary of three shillings per week. The following April she gained a satisfactory report at the inspector's examination and was admitted as a pupil teacher. After four years, in July 1880, Ann went to Edinburgh to sit the entrance examination for 'Training School'.

The log-book does not record her success presumably because she was now considered to have left school but the headmaster of Little Brechin was happy in June 1897 to record that pupil teacher Maggie Mitchell, for whose instruction he had been responsible, had successfully passed the Queen's Scholarship Examination. At Kilry, in the same year there was a sadder story. A pupil teacher, Isabella Cargill, died of acute pneumonia and the headmaster recorded in the log-book 'the great regret of the teacher, the pupils and the community at large'.

The stages in teacher training are well illustrated by the successes of Miss Thomasina Muir who spent her entire teaching career in Fife. (See Appendix 1)

Appointments as head teacher were few in the early years of compulsory education. In 1894 the School Board at Maryton resolved 'as an experiment' to appoint a female teacher, although the neighbouring School Board of Craig had already appointed Mrs Jane Wilkie, a widow, at Westerton School, and Miss Jessie Coull as headmistress of the Infant School at Ferryden. Miss Coull's work over 25 years was so valued that a special memorial was placed in the school on her death in 1912.

The Spiritual Inheritance.

PREACHED IN CRAIG UNITED FREE CHURCH
ON 30th JUNE, 1912.

In Memoriam

MISS COULL,

THE HEAD-MISTRESS OF THE INFANT SCHOOL,
FERRYDEN, WHO DIED ON 27th JUNE, 1912.

A Tablet to her memory, subscribed to by friends and past pupils, was placed in the Infant School, by the permission of the Craig School Board, and was unveiled by Mrs. Stansfeld, Dunninald. On it are these words :—

In Memory of

JESSIE COULL,
FOR 25 YEARS HEAD-MISTRESS
IN THIS SCHOOL.

ENTERED INTO REST, JUNE 28th, 1912.

May perpetual light shine upon her.

ALEXANDER BROTHERS   GLASGOW

10 *Miss Jessie Coull, the headmistress of Ferryden Infant School*

At Rescobie when the head teacher, Mr Simpson retired 'under the age limit' in 1924, his place was taken by the first female head-teacher there, Agnes Allan. From then on, until the school closed, there were only women teachers – Miss Lish, Miss Alice Brown and Miss Mabel Cuthbert. Increasingly in the smaller one-teacher rural schools this became the pattern in Angus.

11 *The little boy in the photograph attended Ferryden Infant School*

Infant Schools in Rural Angus

As early as 1834 an infant school was opened in Ferryden with 84 pupils under six years of age. A school building specifically for these children was built in 1838 by the generosity of Miss Maria Ross of Rossie who pitied the plight of the hard-worked fishermen's wives. In the following year she gave £40 for salary and expenses. The teacher was Miss Petrie, a 'suitable and pious female teacher' in accordance with the strictures of the Director of the Model Infant School in Glasgow, David Stowe, who had advised that 'an Infant Schoolmaster must be decidedly pious'.

The Statistical Account of Glamis of 1836 records that 'a flourishing Infants School opened the previous year attended by about 60 scholars paying 1d. [one old penny] per week'. However in many rural areas infants were catered for in the local school. The head teacher in one such school in 1886 revealed her exasperation in the log-book with 'an infant about 3 years of age who was sent to school this week. She did nothing but make a noise and go about everywhere, thereby impeding the school work'. At the same school almost twenty years later an infant was enrolled causing the teacher to record 'as he is under five and wants too much nursing, have advised his mother to withdraw him till he is five'.

The Rural Schools after 1872

The New School Boards

The School Boards set up by the Education (Scotland) Act had considerable local powers. In Angus there were 60 separate boards with from five to 15 members. Landowners were always represented as were ministers and Kirk Session members. The new headmaster at Kinnell school made a meticulous first entry in his log-book on 20 November 1873 stating that he had 'received the log-book and school board minute book and conscience clause on cardboard and blank timetable on cardboard at 11.50 a.m. from the manservant of Mr. Goodlet, Chairman of the School Board'. Although ladies were eligible to serve, few were elected in Angus although Miss More-Gordon served for many years on the Montrose Landward School Board for Loanhead School.

The boards received a Parliamentary Grant from the Scotch Education Department and could levy a 'School Rate' on local ratepayers which was sometimes the source of much complaint and certainly gave everyone a keen interest in the efficient running of the local school. The local ratepayers at Loanhead/Hillside accepted the £20 increase to £150 per annum in 1892 but many complained about a further increase of £50 the following year pointing out that this represented a rate of 5d. in £1. However at the same time the School Boards of Craig and Logie-Pert felt justified in raising the rate to 10d. in the £1.

As well as maintaining the school and providing a house for the schoolmaster, the Boards appointed and dismissed teachers and fixed salaries. There was no nationally agreed wage.

Education was now compulsory and 'Defaulting Officers' were appointed to ensure attendance. The officer for Craig, Westerton and Ferryden schools in the 1890s was a local man, Alexander Clyne who, in addition to his normal work, reported parents of local absentees to the school board for the sum of £10 per year. He was succeeded by Joseph Coull, a local joiner in Ferryden, who acted as the Craig School Board officer for many years. It was the duty of every parent to provide elementary education in 'the three Rs' for their children between the ages of five and 13. School fees in Angus were usually charged at 9d. per week although help was given to those in need. Each child in a family after the third could be taught free provided the oldest had 90% of attendance. Parents who failed to send their children to school could be prosecuted, the customary penalty being £1 or 14 days imprisonment for every three-month period. School Boards did not hesitate to prosecute. At Invertay School in August 1882 it was recorded 'teacher absent in connection with an action raised against a parent for

KINGOLDRUM.

SCHOOL BOARD.—At a meeting of this Board which was held in the School on Thursday last, Mr Charles Findlay presided, it was resolved to hold the triennial election on Saturday, 14th April, between 12 and 7 P.M. The first meeting of the new Board was fixed for Saturday 21st April. The Board also resolved to have a public meeting in the School for the nomination of candidates on March 29th. The Rev. J. C. Jack was appointed Returning Officer for the ensuing election.

OATHLAW.

SCHOOL BOARD.—The election of a School Board for the parish of Oathlaw takes place in the Schoolroom, Oathlaw, on Saturday. There are six candidates for five seats, the nominations being as follows :—Lieutenant-Colonel Greenhill-Cardyne of Finavon ; Rev. Alexander Ritchie, Oathlaw ; J. S. Falconer, farmer, Bogindollo ; William Ritchie, farmer, Ordie ; James Wilson, farmer, Battledykes ; and John Webster, farmer, Meadows. Mr A. Hay, Forfar, is Returning Officer.

LINTRATHEN.

SCHOOL BOARD MEETING.—On Tuesday evening a meeting of electors was held in the Boardroom for the nomination of candidates for seats in Lintrathen School Board. The election takes place on the 15th March. For the five seats ten candidates have been nominated, viz :— Messrs Thomas Fenton, Foldend ; Robert Easson, West Campsie ; Andrew L. Guthrie, Pitewan ; William Lindsay, Balintore ; George Annand, Reekie Linn House ; Charles Duncan, Macritch ; John Ogilvy, Nether Scythie ; David Stewart, Craigyloch ; David Fenton, Purgavie ; Rev. J. R. Strachan, The Manse. The first five are members of the present Board.

AIRLIE.

SCHOOL BOARD.—Five candidates have been nominated for the five vacant seats at Airlie School Board, and consequently a poll has been averted. The new Board comprise :—Rev. J. F. Linn, Airlie ; Mr H. T. Munro, Lindertis ; Mr Andrew Nicoll, Barns ; Mr T. M. Nicoll, Littleton ; and Wm. Wilson, Airlie.

12 *School Board meetings were reported in the press*

recovery of fees from 9.15a.m. to 11.40a.m. Register of IV Standard was also removed from the school during that time as evidence in the case'. Understandably some rural children came unwillingly to school. If their parents were poor, as many agricultural labourers were, the children were looked upon as extra hands in the fields particularly at harvest time. (See Appendix 3)

The problems facing the teachers in the rural Angus schools are clearly revealed in the log-books kept by every head teacher.

What the School Log-Books Reveal

Attendance

The fact that the school could be granted extra money for satisfactory attendance greatly exercised the minds of all headmasters. They were constantly deploring in the log-books occasions for poor attendance. However, the rural schools of Angus were populated, in the main, by the children of the farms and the fishing communities and the seasons governing farming and fishing caused the number of pupils to fluctuate. There were constant changes among agricultural workers, some of whom changed regularly at 'term time' in November and May. At Kilry in 1908 the headmaster recorded 'Lovely weather but terrible falling off in attendance during the week, perhaps owing to its being the 'Term' week, and the prevalence of manure-spreading'. Children were needed to help at harvest and were therefore absent from class. Potatoes had to be lifted in October and turnips hoed in July. At Aberlemno School in October 1874 the teacher sadly wrote 'hardly know what to do sometimes, the classes are so empty. Potato gathering has more attractions than the school'. At Stracathro in September 1912 it was noted that 'between whooping cough and farmers pushing their work, the school has had a bad time of it for the last three months'. In Padanaram, while the log-book makes no mention of the start of the war in 1914, it does record 'September 25th: The shadow of potato lifting is here. '

13 *The potato harvest at Ferryden*

Local farmers and estate owners had no compunction about employing schoolchildren if their needs required it. At St Vigeans in 1905 the headteacher was sufficiently angered to write 'pupils are being employed as beaters by the Earl of Northesk. The Earl is a member – albeit an absentee member – of the St. Vigeans School Board'! It made no difference for the next year he recorded the same complaint. Similarly at Braes of Coull grouse-driving was the reason for many absences, and in Carroch in September 1908 the teacher remarked 'attendance very bad, Scholars are driving game' while in August 1910 the attendance was very bad 'as the children are engaged on the hill raising the birds for the shooting tenant at Pearsie'. At Rescobie in 1908 the teacher wrote that 'berry picking is the excuse for low attendance'. In February 1913 there was a request from the Clerk of Kingoldrum School Board to the headteacher at Carroch to allow a girl leave of absence for one month for tree planting'. The teacher at Kilry showed his frustration with the blatant disregard for school requirements in 1914. 'Game-beating on the Bamff Estate. All the boys in the Senior-room absent notwithstanding the fact that the school holidays are arranged to suit the Berry-picking and Potato gathering. A little wholesome authority required by the S. Board'. He must have been further upset in April 1916 to receive an unexpected visit from the HMI on the day of a cattle-sale at Alyth. The inspector solemnly noted the poor attendance as the headteacher explained that many boys were employed as cattle drivers for the day.

Some pupils were kept at home to look after smaller children when, for example as at Little Brechin in 1896 'mothers are engaged turnip thinning'. Pupils could be out of school for months at a time making the teacher's job all the more difficult. (See Appendix 3)

At a time when many children walked three or more miles to school from the age of four or five severe weather could cause major problems. An interesting survey reported in the Carmyllie School log-book in 1882 states, 'of 82 children, 4 have a road 'all the way' to the school, 28 part of the way, 40 no road, and 10 from the village'. Although it is claimed that weather patterns are changing, throughout the period covered by the log-books there is evidence of heavy rain, flooding and snowstorms from time to time. The Carroch log-book records that on 21 February 1879 'a snow storm of unprecedented severity has prevailed in the district during the whole week. It is said that such a depth of snow has not been seen for at least 40 years'. An entry in May 1913 at Rescobie records 'this has been a week of excessive rain … the loch is up on the road, so that no child can get to or from school dry shod'. In December 1938 at Padanaram 'only 28 pupils were present and most have wet feet'. At Kilry in wartime in December 1944 'many children have heavy colds as it is impossible for them to get to school with their feet dry. Very few have wellingtons and the boots available in the shops only last a few days in wet weather'.

In February 1947 the heavy snow blocked roads and school was closed for weeks on and off – 'school opened on the 17th. March but roads dangerous for smaller children owing to high banks of snow and narrow opening for traffic'. Teachers were sometimes concerned that poor attendance would reflect on their achievements and, knowing the log-book would be read by visiting inspectors, made their excuses in advance – 'I do most heartily wish the weather would improve else we can NOT be prepared for the Annual inspection'.

However a poor attendance had its benefits also as the teacher at Tannadice pointed out in March 1899:

> *A severe storm of frost and snow accounts for the low attendance. Generally the backward pupils are absent at such times. Consequently the work has gone on smoothly this week.*

There were happier reasons for non-attendance when, for one reason or another, a holiday was granted. At Kilry in August 1883 pupils had a holiday to attend the annual gathering of the 'Glenisla Highland and Friendly Society'. Until the nineteen twenties there were no official holiday dates. Even Christmas was a school day with only 'a section of the community keeping Christmas'. School treats until after World War I were usually in January, a celebration of 'Auld Yule' At Kingoldrum on

---

PADANARAM.

SCHOOL TREAT.—The children attending the school were entertained on Friday evening to their annual treat. There was a large attendance of children and adults. Amongst those present were :—Mr and Mrs Carrie, Balindarg ; Mr and Mrs Lyon, Drumgley ; Mr and Mrs Ogilvy, Balinshoe ; Mrs Anderson, Redford ; Miss Chalmers, Miss Knox, Miss Eggie, &c. An interesting and harmonious programme of songs, games, and dances, supplimented by a series of limelight views, was, gone through. Special credit is due to Mr and Mrs Fairweather and the many ladies and gentlemen who left nothing undone for the enjoyment of the company. A pleasant evening was brought to a close with the usual votes of thanks and the singing of the National Anthemn and ' Auld Lang Syne.'

SCHOOL TREAT.—Through the kindness of Mrs Ogilvy, the Glenprosen School children —to the number of about forty—had their annual treat given them on Wednesday evening. A number of parents accompanied the children, who met at Balnaboth for tea at four o'clock. After partaking of a hearty tea in the hall, nicely decorated for the occasion, an adjournment was made to the library, where suitable presents were given out to the delight of the recipients. They again returned to the hall, where dancing and singing were engaged in till about ten o'clock, when the party broke up, all highly pleased with their night's enjoyment. Before separating, the usual votes of thanks were heartily accorded.

14 *Auld Yule celebrations at Padanarum and Glenprosen*

Christmas Day in 1922 'after giving and getting little gifts between pupils and teachers the school was dismissed at one o'clock' thus enabling the teacher to claim a 'double attendance'. Summer holidays accommodated the needs of the farmers. At St Vigeans by 12 August 1873 the pupils were in no mood for work. The headmaster recorded, 'received a numerously signed petition for the vacation — refused'. The next day he found 'some heads of ripe barley laid on my desk but paid no attention to them'. On 14 August he felt there 'was No work worth speaking of unless it is in my own hands. Finally he gave in. 'Plainly see it is no use going against public opinion any longer and give the vacation.' Agricultural concerns meant that in 1883 Carroch school would close for 'the Agricultural Show at Kirriemuir' and also for 'the Muckle Market'.

Many schools had a summer outing and the headmaster in Carroch in June 1889 justified a two day holiday since 'the trip to Clova on Tuesday was most enjoyable' and on the next day 'the scholars would not be in a good condition for work'. Unfortunately when Kinnell School had a trip to Lunan Bay in July 1891 'after the carts started it came on very rainy. On the whole the affair was not a success. The children cannot have been very comfortable but no accident occurred'. By 1946, school outings had become more sophisticated. The Rescobie children at Christmas time had an exciting trip to the local cinema in Forfar by bus to see the matinee performance of Walt Disney's 'Make Mine Music'.

Other obligational holidays at a time when ministers were always on the School Board were Sacramental Fast Days. Whether the pupils spent the holiday appropriately is not recorded.

It is possible to trace the path of a travelling circus which each year journeyed throughout Perthshire and Angus by looking at the school logbooks. One headmaster after another records that the excitement of seeing a parade of elephants, camels, clowns and acrobats proved too great a temptation for many. In 1880 at St Thomas School 'so many were absent in the afternoon since a circus has come to town that I did not take the roll'. At Carroch, with a circus arrived at Kirriemuir, 'an unofficial holiday was taken by many'.

There was a temptation for teachers seeking the higher grant for attendance to falsify registers. The keeping of a correct register assumed a fantastic degree of importance. Registers must be marked at the beginning of both morning and afternoon with each name space filled with an **o** or an **x**. Each child stood to answer, "Present". Members of the School Board regularly checked and signed the registers and it was not uncommon for an inspector to turn up unexpectedly to hold a spot check. Falsifying

15 *Extract from Inverkeilor Public School register, 1906*

* The age of the pupil on the last day of the sixth month of the financial year settles the age-group to which he belongs. A pupil whose seventh birthday falls on or before that day is counted for the year as being "Between 7 and 10;" one who is seven on or after the following day is classed for the year with children "Under 7." (Art. 19 B. 1).

Signatures of School Managers
with date of visit, and
NOTES BY TEACHER.

No.	Name		
41			
42			
43	James Hamilton		
44	Geo. Fenig		
45	Geo. Mollison		
46	Wm Ross		
47	Alex Stephen		
48	Gordid Petrishie		
49	John Simonde		
50	Robt Foster		
51	Alex Smart		
52	Peter Smith		
53	Andrew Fyfa		
54	Alex Watson		
55	David Whytie		
56	Charles McGregO		
57	David Fyfa		
58	William Mitchell		
59	Alex Lawton		
60	Thos Johnston		

Total Attendances up to Date (brought forward): 268 · 302 · 307

No. on Roll: 39 · 39 · 39

the register could lead to suspension or even the sack. At Carmyllie West School in 1876 the Inspector's report was very critical stating,

> As the teacher has entirely disregarded the regulations issued by this Department on the subject of registration and which are printed in the registers which have actually been used by him, and as the Returns upon which the calculation of the grant depends are found to be entirely untrustworthy, My Lords must refuse to allow the payment of any Grant.

As you can imagine the School Board was far from pleased!

With considerable pleasure therefore teachers in Angus seem to have enjoyed recording a series of official holidays. The closing stages of the Boer war provided an excellent excuse for celebration. March 1900 marked the relief of Ladysmith. On 1st June Lord Roberts entered Johannesburg while 3 days later schools closed again to celebrate the capture of Pretoria. The headmaster at Inverkeilor was more reluctant to close the school on such occasions but even he recorded 'on Wednesday owing to the capture of Pretoria only 29% of children came to school. School was therefore dismissed at 3.30 p.m.' Curiously there are fewer mentions of holidays after the two World Wars. But in February 1918 at Rescobie 'the school was closed on Friday to permit arrangements to be made for an entertainment in aid of War funds'. Just six months later 'to celebrate peace the King recommended Education authorities to grant all children an extension of summer holidays'. In 1945 there was no extended holiday granted but most schools noted a special VE Holiday to celebrate victory in Europe. For example at Kilry on 8th May 1945 the head teacher recorded enthusiastically

> This is "V.E. Day". Germany has unconditionally surrendered to the Allies and the Prime minister gave official confirmation of the cessation of hostilities at 3 p.m. School is closed on V.E. Day and the two days following.

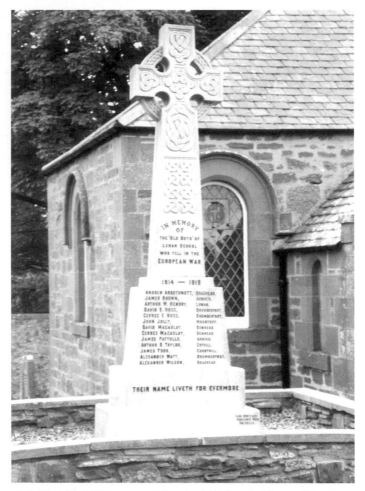

16 *First World War memorial to the 'Old Boys' of Lunan School*

Discipline: Rewards and Punishments

The Education Act of 1872 was described as 'education for employment on lower class lines' but it did lay the groundwork for literacy and in some ways reached a very high standard. This was achieved in spite of problems which today's teachers would not tolerate for a moment. The great influx after 1872 of pupils, unwilling in many cases, meant that teachers were often handling not just one problem child but often large numbers of children of varying ages in the one class. At Carnoustie in 1887 the headmaster records that 'The Third and Fourth Standards contain 73 pupils. Up till now they have been taught by J. Ferguson, 4th. Year pupil-teacher. He is overweighted with this number'. Poor lad! He must have faced considerable problems. This partly accounts for the strict discipline and heavy emphasis on corporal punishment that seems to have been the norm in urban schools although this had always been a feature of Scottish education. In the rural schools the log-books do not reveal many instances of severe punishment although older people often refer to the heavy use of the tawse as common practice.

At Little Brechin, in 1880, James, of Standard IV 'received three strokes of the tawse for throwing stones'. In 1890, another truant pupil at Little Brechin got a severe thrashing when he returned the following day. The teacher at Carroch had difficulties in 1897 when he

> had occasion to punish a boy in Standard VI for leaving at the interval – 3 o'clock yesterday without asking permission. He at first refused to submit to punishment, saying his father ordered him not to do so as he, the father, could take his boy out of school when he liked.

The same boy was later punished severely for stealing the dinner of one of the girls. Parents sometimes felt their children had been unfairly dealt with. For instance one entry explains that 'two scholars, brother and sister, left in the middle of the week because I had to punish the boy pretty sharply for bad conduct'. Bullying was not confined to the boys. One teacher records,

> had to severely reprimand some of the bigger girls for ill-using the youngest ones on the way home from school, and by rough careless play knocking some of them over in the playground and hurting them a good deal.

In general teachers seem to have used the tawse less on girls than boys. At Carmyllie West the boys involved probably felt hard done by in 1878 for the teacher marking a written history examination recorded,

> As each pupil had got a separate list of questions, copying was rendered impossible from each other ... I found that many of the papers had the exact words used in the text book ... On Wednesday settled the matter by admonishing the girls, and giving

each boy, guilty of setting so bad an example and lowering the moral tone of the
school, six lashes over the palm of the hand with the leathering tawse.

Some pupils were prepared to stand up to and defy authority. Others were notorious for wrongdoing. In the Monifieth log-book it is possible to pursue the school career of John Duncan over several years as he played truant, left his books exposed to the wind and rain, encouraged other children to defy authority, threw a dart which struck another pupil on the neck and generally earned the title of 'a notorious case'. The headteacher records in 1888 that

> *doors of the outhouses in the boys' playground were cut and otherwise defaced.*
> *Though enquiry was made no one could be found willing to point out the delinquent.*
> *The marks were all obliterated with paint that no example might be left for invitation*
> *and that any fresh mark might be detected.*

The teacher had his suspicions – 'The initials J.D. pointed to a boy in the Mixed Department'.

A curious punishment was tried at Inverarity where a notorious truant who had 'been warned, admonished and punished before for the same fault' was 'shut up in the lavatory for two hours with a task in writing beside corporal punishment'. At Friockheim a boy called John found himself in real trouble in 1894 when he

> *mounted the dividing wall of the playground, looked into the girl's latrines and*
> *thereafter threw stones at the girls while they were sitting on them. Such an offence*
> *could not be overlooked and on his refusing to accept punishment was expelled.*

The dominie at Stracathro in 1933 does not record exactly what happened to the 'seven boys who had been snowballing' who 'came in a quarter of an hour late and were punished'.

A main reason for rigid control must have been the dreaded visits of Her Majesty's Inspectors. The time of the annual inspection was an incredibly anxious one. Payment of the grant was entirely dependent on the success or failure of the pupils. Extra money came from a satisfactory attendance record and bonuses were given for singing and discipline amounting to one shilling per pupil for a satisfactory performance and one shilling and sixpence for an excellent one. Any teacher can imagine the feverish preparation beforehand and the frantic drilling in the '3 Rs' with threats to secure exemplary behaviour. Obviously the examination results, published in the local newspaper, reflected well or badly on the teacher and prospects of promotion could be very much affected. Inspections could by no means be taken for granted In the 1899 report on St Vigeans School the inspector wrote in the log-book

> *As a result of the said inspection I have to report that the teacher, Mr. Wm.,*
> *Crockhart, is responsible for the unsatisfactory state of the school and therefore*
> *declare him incompetent, unfit and inefficient.*

Certificate of Merit.

(ARTICLE 29 OF THE SCOTCH CODE.)

THE LORDS OF THE COMMITTEE OF THE PRIVY COUNCIL ON EDUCATION IN SCOTLAND have been pleased to award this Certificate of Merit in terms of Article 29 of the Scotch Code to _Lizzie Green,_ a pupil over fourteen years of age in _Inverkeitor Public School_

It is certified (*a*) that the holder was shown to the satisfaction of His Majesty's Inspector to have been of good proficiency in the ordinary subjects of an elementary education before enrolment in a Supplementary Course, (*b*) that she has been under instruction in a Supplementary Course for not less than one complete school year, (*c*) that her general progress in the work of the Course was _Good_

The holder's character and conduct are certified to by the Headmaster, and the marks which, in the opinion of the Headmaster and Class Teacher, represent her attainments in the various subjects of instruction are shown on the back of this Certificate.

The issue of this CERTIFICATE is authorised by the SCOTCH EDUCATION DEPARTMENT on or after 1 AUGUST 1905

J. Struthers

A.—Subjects common to all Supplementary Courses.		B.—Subjects of Head B., Schedule V. of the Code.	
English	Good	Laws of Health	Good
Arithmetic	Good	The Commerce & History &	Very Good
Mark to be assigned for Handwriting	Good	Nature Study, Drill, Singing	Good

C.—Special Subjects selected under Schedule VI. of the Code.

Special Course.

Mensuration &		Good
Drawing		Good
Needlework		Good

WE CERTIFY that the foregoing marks represent our opinion of the holder's proficiency in the various subjects of instruction as judged by the whole character of her work in each subject, and that her character and conduct have been _Very Good_.

Chas Crawford { Class Teacher. / Head Teacher.

Countersigned on behalf of the Managers of the School,

W B & L (x) —23762 - 5000-8-4

17 *School certificate*

Scotch Education Department

MERIT CERTIFICATE.

The Lords of the Committee of the Privy Council on Education in Scotland, Hereby Certify that *Christina Nicoll* a Scholar in the *Kirkden Public* School, having Been examined in *June* 189 *9* has shown thorough proficiency in Reading, Writing, Arithmetic and English according to the requirements for the Merit Certificate, and has received efficient instruction in an approved curriculum of studies embracing the following subjects :-

Geography   *British History*

H. Craik Secretary

I Certify that *Christina Nicoll*'s character and conduct have been entirely satisfactory
Age last birthday 13 years.   *James Downs.* Head Master.

18 *School Certificate of Christina Nicoll, a pupil at Kirkden School (see opposite)*

No wonder teachers were prepared to wield the tawse to avoid a report like that!

Discipline might also be improved and hard work encouraged by the presentation of prizes. After the school inspector's 'visit' prizes were usually given to all who passed. In 1879 one teacher went a step further. 'Gave a little book to all who passed at last Inspection; and a smaller one to the others to induce, further and increase perseverance.' At Logie Pert and Maryton, Edinburgh Angus prizes were awarded to 'the best boy and the best girl in the school'. Very often the School Board would offer small prizes for encouragement. At Panbride there was a drawing prize. At Cortachy Lady Airlie gave a special sewing prize each year while at Rescobie the Chairman of the School Board gave two prizes in 1909 for wild flower collections. Good attendance often merited a special certificate for each year. Perfect attendance for several years might earn a book with a suitable inscription. During the Second World War treats and rewards were limited. At Stracathro in 1941 'owing to the war the scholars didn't have their usual Xmas treat, not even a tea. For a change each child was given a good helping of Xmas pudding, and an orange'. Even when the war ended the effects of rationing or a shortage of money were still affecting prize giving. A log-book entry for 1947 at Braes of Coull states 'prizes were presented to the children in the form of tennis balls, books being out of the question' !

The headmaster at Monikie in the 1920s encouraged good attendance but also benefited himself by dismissing school half an hour early on a Friday each week 100% attendance was achieved. It is not difficult to imagine the pupil wrath visited on anyone who, for no good reason, spoiled the record.

Sometimes the master felt he had to be firm with staff as well as pupils. The new headteacher at Kinnettles in 1919 reprimanded 'Miss S.' stating 'I have again found it necessary to call her attention to the spitting on slates. Every child should have a sponge and water for the purpose of cleaning slates'. Poor 'Miss S.' !

19 *Kirkden School*

Curriculum

Educationalists over the years have searched for the most suitable curriculum for primary children. When, James Currie, the Principal of the Church of Scotland Training College, Edinburgh, wrote the *Principles and Practice of Common School Education*, used by generations of Normal School students, he listed the subjects to be 'imparted', as 'language, number and writing' but he did not stop there. 'General knowledge, … laws of health … knowledge of the mind … social knowledge … geography and history are also included in the curriculum' as well as drawing and singing.

His views had much influence on the new School Code of 1873 which laid down what a Board School education should be. After infants, there were six standards laid down in Reading, Writing and Arithmetic plus work in History and Geography for Standards 4, 5, and 6. (See Appendix 4) The reading syllabus shows a reading progression with an increasing emphasis on formal grammar. All head teachers were encouraged to pay close attention to the standards required because of the system of Payment by Results.

20 *A Ferryden pupil's jotter from 1876*

The award of a government grant to a school was directly related to the degree of success shown by its pupils at the annual HMI inspection. The effect of this was not altogether good. A pupil could only be presented once for examination at a particular Standard. Even if he/she failed the pupil had to be put forward the following year at the next Higher Standard. Therefore brighter pupils might be held back even if they were fit to proceed to a higher lever. The dull ones, if successful, could earn the school as much in grant as the clever ones. Pupils were driven to do well by rote learning, daily drill in reading and arithmetic and of course corporal punishment.

In 1946 in the Advisory Council's Report on Primary Education there was the following statement: 'We discard with little regret the narrow and obsolete view that reading, writing and arithmetic are the three fundamentals of education.' The report continued, 'The curriculum and methods of the primary school should be thought out afresh.' The Primary Memorandum of 1965 was the result of this approach. The Consultative Committee on the Curriculum in 1986 published a report which described the curriculum as being 'organised under the broad headings of language arts, environmental studies, aspects of expressive arts, mathematics and religious education' More recently the 5 to 14 Guidelines have formed the basis of the curriculum.

If we read the log-books of the Angus rural schools we discover that, as well as the basics, some teachers in these small establishments, in spite of the many problems they faced, managed to teach an amazing variety of subjects. Primary children today would be amazed to be expected to do what a Friockheim boy achieved in 1834: 'Dauvit Croall, son of John Croall, grocer, could read his Latin Bible from beginning to end.' In one rural school in 1883 the highest Latin class had begun to read the First Book of the odes of Horace! At Kinnell School in May 1875 the teacher wrote 'I have begun to hear Latin and Geometry classes from 8 to 9 in the morning'.

The first steps in reading for the rural school child in the nineteenth century usually began by learning the letters of the alphabet from what was known as *The Penny Book*, which tried to teach moral lessons as well as knowledge of the alphabet. A Glenesk version contained the following verses.

> **B**: *Be sure your letters for to learn*
> *And what your parents say.*
> *And every night and every morn*
> *To God most fervent pray.*
>
> **D**: *Depart from those who'er you know*
> *To steal, to swear or lie.*
> *For those that lead a wicked life*
> *Must be afraid to die.*

Since there was usually one reading book per Standard after 1873, the bright pupils soon became bored as the same work was read over and over again while others might well be encouraged by an anxious teacher to memorise if they could not read. There are no references in the log-books of teachers providing supplementary material but this must have happened fairly often. In 1894 in one small rural school the harassed new teacher wrote 'ordered new books as the books of the 14 pupils present were all different. Hinders work'. The gift of library books for schools must have been well received. In 1908 at Little Brechin 'a handsome bookcase of about 180 books from Mr. James Coats Jnr., Ferguslie House, Paisley' was gratefully noted. Inspectors often noted with disapproval the practice of children moving a finger along the line of text in the reading book. An 1888 report states 'fingering should be eradicated both in the lower and higher classes'.

21 *A slate with pencil box*

Writing in the early years was done on slates for paper was expensive and a slate could be wiped clean again and again. But once in Standard 3 a pupil would be exercised regularly to produce a good style of copperplate handwriting. There is little evidence of creative writing before the 1950s, but from early on Dictation seems to have played a major part with the teacher at Pitkennedy noting in 1885 'the Dictation Exercises in the 3rd. Standard have been very unsatisfactory on several occasions recently. Punished for it'.

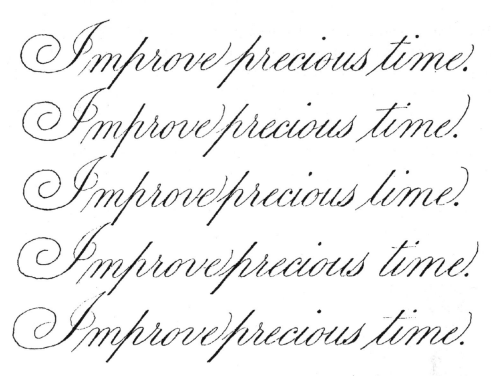

Improve precious time.
Improve precious time.
Improve precious time.
Improve precious time.
Improve precious time.

22 *A page from a pupil's exercise book showing the high standard which could be achieved*

Arithmetic certainly held an important place in the day's lessons. In Little Brechin an entry in 1884 reads :

> *Standard VI now fairly begun to Fractions*
> *Standard V to Practice*
> *Standard IV to Compound Rules*
> *Standard III to Multiplication*

Eleven years later the same teacher records 'Standard III is now fairly master of Long Division, much time has been spent drilling in short division'.

In the early years of compulsory education text books often tried to inculcate moral lesson, even in arithmetic, as this sample in *Sums of Capacity* from Ferryden shows:

> *Two pints will make one quart*
> *Four quarts one gallon strong.*
> *Some drink too little, some too much.*
> *To drink too much is wrong.*

There was always a great stress laid on mental arithmetic for this could be vital for a good shop worker or clerk if not for the average farm worker. Multiplication rules in a text book of 1880 offer ways of mentally multiplying by 142 and $6/7$! At the beginning of the 20th century in the little school at Carroch 'addition and subtraction of fractions' was being taught to Standard V and 'mental arithmetic cards' were being

(5.) To multiply by 125.

As $125 = \dfrac{1000}{8}$, affix three ciphers, and divide by 8.

$$685 \times 125 = \frac{685\,000}{8} = 85\,625.$$

$$387\,000 \times 125 = \frac{387\,000\,000}{8} = 48\,375\,000.$$

(6.) To multiply by 250.

As $250 = \dfrac{1000}{4}$, affix three ciphers, and divide by 4.

$$763 \times 250 = \frac{763\,000}{4} = 190\,750.$$

(7.) To multiply by $333\frac{1}{3}$.

As $333\frac{1}{3} = \dfrac{1000}{3}$, affix three ciphers, and divide by 3.

$$683 \times 333\frac{1}{3} = \frac{683\,000}{3} = 227\,666\frac{2}{3}.$$

If the sum of the digits in the multiplicand here is divisible by 3 without a remainder, the last three figures in the answer are ciphers; if there is 1 over, they are $333\frac{1}{3}$, if 2, $666\frac{2}{3}$; *e.g.*,—

$$963 \times 333\frac{1}{3} = 321\,000.$$
$$541 \times 333\frac{1}{3} = 180\,333\frac{1}{3}.$$
$$764 \times 333\frac{1}{3} = 254\,666\frac{2}{3}.$$

(8.) To multiply by $142\frac{6}{7}$.

As $142\frac{6}{7} = \dfrac{1000}{7}$, affix three ciphers, and divide by 7.

$$896 \times 142\frac{6}{7} = \frac{896\,000}{7} = 128\,000.$$

$$743 \times 142\frac{6}{7} = \frac{743\,000}{7} = 106\,142\frac{6}{7}.$$

(9.) To multiply by $111\frac{1}{9}$.

As $111\frac{1}{9} = \dfrac{1000}{9}$, affix three ciphers, and divide by 9.

$$675 \times 111\frac{1}{9} = \frac{675\,000}{9} = 75\,000.$$

$$832 \times 111\frac{1}{9} = \frac{832\,000}{9} = 92\,444\frac{4}{9}.$$

Where the sum of the digits in the multiplicand here is divisible by 9, the last three figures in the result are ciphers; where, in dividing by 9, the remainder is 1, they are $111\frac{1}{9}$; where 2, $222\frac{2}{9}$; where 3, $333\frac{1}{3}$; where 4, $444\frac{4}{9}$, and so on.

23 *Some helpful hints for multiplication*

used in Standards III and IV. In Rescobie in March 1906 the teacher records 'special drill in mental arithmetic in both divisions of the school'. One boy in Braes of Coull went out of his way to produce an excuse for his poor test result in 1949. 'Boy did badly in arithmetic – owing to the results of being in a motor smash, having a heavy cold and a sore right eye' !

Learning tables was accorded such importance that in 1881 at St Vigeans the teacher wrote 'tables very badly known throughout the school. Obliged to spend half an hour each day in simultaneous repetition'. Dominies, anxious to do well in inspections, regularly examined the pupils throughout the school. At Carnoustie in 1888 the log records

> *Examination on paper to V and VI Standards. At same time examined Standard III in Grammar. The Grammar of Standard V continues to improve. But the work of Standard VI is much destroyed by the entry against pressure in schoolwork.*

Obviously the teacher was finding it difficult to interest boys who would soon be leaving school and, feeling very frustrated, he continued, 'it is even a trouble to Standard VI boys to stand, they have been so urged on to laziness'! Girls always seem to have been more amenable and, as seems to happen today also, regularly outperformed boys in many subjects. At Little Brechin in 1879 the teacher held a spelling competition for Standard IV. 'Gave 96 words. The girls did pretty well. The boys made a very bad job.'

In Standard IV pupils began formal lessons in History and Geography but even here rote learning was the norm with children learning the names and dates of the Kings and Queens of Scotland. However in 1890 at Carroch the dominie misunderstood the requirements as regards History. 'Under the new code History and Geography being separate and history not being considered obligatory, intend no longer to teach it as a class subject for the purpose of earning a grant.' A year later, perhaps as a result of an Inspector's visit, he wrote, 'Schedule of History to be taught in this school as a class subject'. As late as 1929 we find an HMI in one rural school insisting 'in History the memorising of the main facts should be more emphasised'. At Padanaram pupils would learn by rote the capes, islands and mountains of Scotland and be able to chant together the rivers of the North East, 'The Dee, the Don and the Dev-e-ron'.

Religious instruction formed a regular part of the school day. The shorter catechism, all 107 questions and answers, was faithfully committed to memory, and regular examinations in religious knowledge were held. There was always a minister on the School Board who could be relied upon to take a keen interest. In 1899 the Rev J W Foyer, Minister of Kilry and Chairman of the school board of Glenisla 'warmly commended the appearance made by the pupils in the various Religious subjects'. Forty five years later at Kilry the situation had not changed a great deal.

At the request of Councillor Inglis school was closed today, 9th. June 1944, at dinner-time. The half holiday was a reward for the children's ready answers by Rev. Mr. Reaper on their knowledge of scripture taught during the year.

There is frequent mention in the log-books of singing lessons probably because a special grant was given for music if a child could learn songs by heart and sing them unaccompanied. Usually the only instrument available was a tuning fork, a tonic Sol-Fa modulator the only aid and the songs would be learned line by line. At a time when

In the year 1818, workmen engaged in clearing the foundations for a new church, among the ruins of Dunfermline Abbey, came upon the tomb of Robert the Bruce. A leaden case, shaped at the head into the form of a crown, enclosed the body. Fragments of a rich cloth of gold, which had been spread over it, were still visible. On examining the skeleton, it was found that the ribs of the left breast had been sawn asunder, that the heart might be taken out. The jaw had been

THE BODY OF ROBERT THE BRUCE ENCASED IN LEAD
Discovered at Dunfermline in 1818

fractured at the chin, as the knitted bone showed—doubtless in some hazard of battle. Men looked with wonder and awe upon the skull where once had dwelt counsel so sage and high, and upon the mouldering bone which had once been the strong right arm that had struck down the fierce Bohun.

QUESTIONS.—How long had Bruce been engaged in the national struggle? With what result? What had injured his constitution? Where did he retire? What pursuits occupied the intervals of relief? For whom did he send when he saw that death was near? What did he charge them to do? What was his dying charge to Lord James Douglas? What reason did he give for making the request? What did Douglas reply? What did Bruce say would enable him to die in peace? When did he die? At what age? What effect had his death on the country? Where was he buried? With what ceremony? Who accompanied Douglas on his journey? Where did he carry the King's heart? In what war did he engage on his way? Where was a battle fought? What command was intrusted to Douglas? What was the effect of the Scottish charge? What mistake did the Scots make? What was the result? What did Douglas do and say as he made his last onset? What was done with his body? What was done with the heart of Bruce? What discovery was made at Dunfermline in 1818? In what was the body enclosed? How was it shaped at the head? What did the ribs of the left breast show? Of what did the jaw-bone give evidence?

24 *Scottish history was taught as part of the curriculum after 1872*

Q. 19. What is the misery of that estate whereinto man fell ?

A. All mankind, by their fall, lost communion with God, are under His wrath and curse, and so made liable to all miseries in this life, to death itself, to the pains of hell for ever.

Q. 20. Did God leave all mankind to perish in the estate of sin and misery ?

A. God having, out of His mere good pleasure, from all eternity, elected some to everlasting life, did enter into a covenant of grace, to deliver them out of the estate of sin and misery, and to bring them into a state of salvation by a Redeemer.

Q. 21. Who is the Redeemer of God's elect?

A. The only Redeemer of God's elect is the Lord Jesus Christ, who, being the eternal Son of God, became man, and so was, and continueth to be, God and man in two distinct natures, and one person, for ever.

Q. 22. How did Christ, being the Son of God, become man ?

A. Christ, the Son of God, became man by taking to Himself a true body and a reasonable soul, being conceived by the power of the Holy Ghost, in the womb of the Virgin Mary, and born of her, yet without sin.

25 *Some questions from the Shorter Catechism*

there were no fixed holidays one feels for the headmaster at Carmyllie on a hot day in July 1880 when he recorded 'Heat becoming almost insupportable. Taught the song, *Give me a draught from the crystal spring'*.

THE CRYSTAL SPRING.

From "Hastings' Juvenile Songs."

Give me a draught from the crystal spring, When the

burning sun is high; When the rocks and the woods their

sha - dows fling, Where the pearls and the peb - bles

lie, Where the pearls and the peb-bles lie.

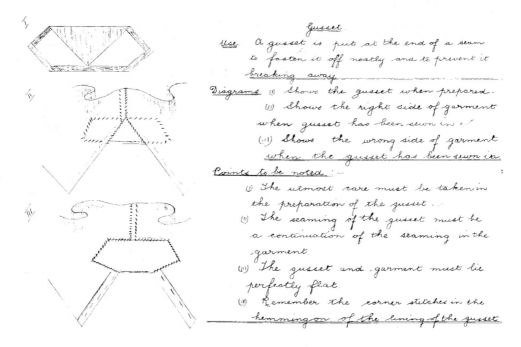

Gusset.

Use A gusset is put at the end of a seam to fasten it off neatly and to prevent it breaking away.

Diagrams (I) Shows the gusset when prepared.
(II) Shows the right side of garment when gusset has been sewn in
(III) Shows the wrong side of garment when the gusset has been sewn in

Points to be noted:—
(I) The utmost care must be taken in the preparation of the gusset.
(II) The seaming of the gusset must be a continuation of the seaming in the garment
(III) The gusset and garment must lie perfectly flat.
(IV) Remember the corner stitches in the hemming on of the lining of the gusset

26 *Extract from a student teacher's workbook*

In 1888 the headmaster records 'the following songs were prepared for the inspection which was held yesterday.

> *1. Rosalie the Prairie Flower*
>
> *2. Ring the Bell Watchman*
>
> *3. The Crystal Spring*
>
> *4. They're Coming Home Today*
>
> *5. Bonnie ran the Burnie Doon*
>
> *6. Scotland and her Queen*

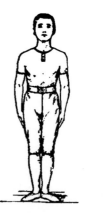

27 *Physical exercises*

Since girls were expected to become good housewives there was always an emphasis on useful domestic tasks. Yet in a small rural community such instruction was valued even if it meant staying late. A typical log-book entry states:

Cookery and laundry classes have been held in the school this week – till the end of the month. To enable these classes to meet at 4 o'clock the interval for dinner has been curtailed and the school closed half an hour earlier.

The closest most children came to any kind of study of science subjects was the Object Lesson . One teacher in November 1884 seems to have covered a surprising variety of topics in one week. 'Gave object lessons to infants – the ostrich, the whale, the tigger [sic] the horse.'

A manual was provided for physical training but the subject was normally referred to as drill and this seems to have been an apt description for the series of military style exercises were designed to help to inculcate obedience, not so much to devclop the body as subdue the spirit! Children usually entered and left school marching and sometimes singing as the dominie beat time. The more generous School Boards supplied dumb bells and bar bells. Sometimes the headmaster would drill the whole school in the playground. A curious entry in the Keptie School Log for 1895 records:

THE COW.

WHAT is this? The picture of a cow. What do you mean by the picture of a cow? The likeness of the cow.
What is the cow? What kind of animal? A beast. Name some other kinds of animals. Birds, fishes, insects, and reptiles.
What is the difference between a beast and a fish? Beasts live on the land, and fishes in the water.
What beasts can live either on land or in water? The otter, etc.
Where do birds live? In the air.
What does the cow eat? Have all animals the same food? What food do birds use generally? The seeds of plants. With what do they pick up the seeds? With their bill.
On what do some birds live? On the flesh of other animals. What are birds of this kind called? Birds of prey.
Are there any beasts that kill and eat other animals? What are they called? Beasts of prey.
Is the cow a beast of prey? Why not? What other animals, besides the cow, feed on grass? Rabbits.

28 *Example of an object lesson*

The Drill has taken place in the playground, but at 2.30 rain interfered with the instruction and the girls of the 6th. Standard and the ex-sixth got separate lessons in the Boys' Lavatory.

By 1936 things had moved on and the Rescobie teacher had a day off 'to attend the Pavilion Theatre, Forfar to see exhibition of films showing classes being taught according to the department's 1933 Syllabus of Physical Instruction'. Two months later 'Apparatus for Physical Training was received'.

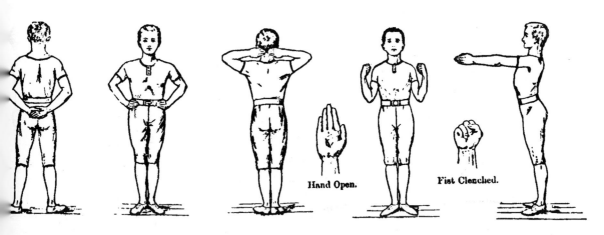

Hand Open.   Fist Clenched.

The log-book for Stracathro School, like many others, records in 1945 that 'books and stationary are now supplied free'.

Needlework Drill.

1. Hold the needle between the thumb and forefinger of the left hand, as if for threading.

2. Put the eye of the needle into the top of the thimble, and then take hold of it with the right-hand forefinger and thumb well down towards the point.

3. Make the stitch (putting the needle only a little way in).

4. Keep all the fingers still, and let the right thumb hop on to the top joint of the *left* forefinger, close to, but at a right angle with the other thumb.

5. Push the needle quite in.

6. Let the thumb and forefinger take hold of the needle, and the thimble finger go up a little, but keep the other two down. When the cotton is pulled out rather more than an inch, let the thimble finger fall on it and keep it tightly letting it rest on the third finger while you finish pulling it out.

Great care must be taken to keep the needle in the thimble till after No. 5 is finished.

The above directions are for the teachers to refer to

29 *Needlework Drill*

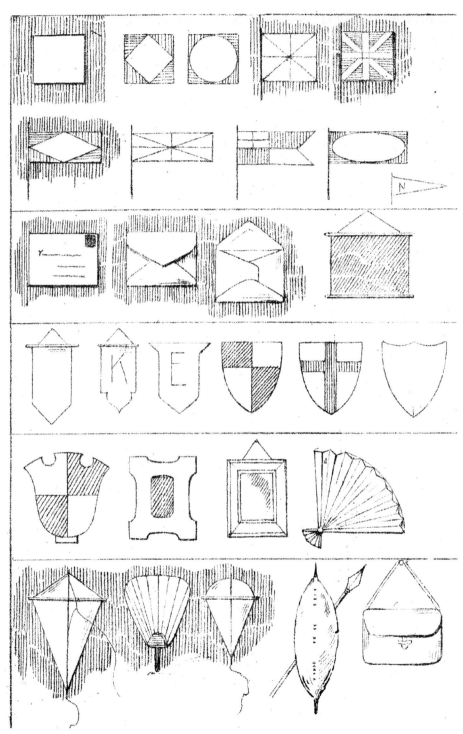

30 *From a drawing scheme for schools introduced in 1910*

Health, Hygiene and School Dinners

The log-books reveal that in some areas in the 19th century, where there might be no indoor sanitation at home, young rural children were often ignorant of basic hygiene and the advantages of flush toilets. This entry of the dominie at Inverkeilor in 1899 is not unusual, 'am trying to get the boys of the infant Room and Standard I to use the urinals instead of more exposed places'.

Even in rural districts cases of serious infections occurred from time to time. Scarlet fever, diphtheria and whooping cough are frequently mentioned and in the early years of compulsory education outbreaks of typhoid are noted. In 1878 and again in 1883 the school at Little Brechin closed because of the prevalence of typhoid and measles and two deaths were recorded. More curiously in July 1883 a number of children are absent from water pox. A child at Kilry school was treated for Typhoid Fever at Forfar Hospital in 1913. Scarlet fever affected even the teacher's family at Carroch in 1886 and when the school closed for three weeks

> *Christina and Isabella Doig came back and removed their slates saying they were going to Kingoldrum school till this one reopened.*

At Inverbrothock in 1913 a decision was taken to close the school

> *after another outbreak of scarlet fever, Great attention has been paid to disinfecting slates. All pictures have been removed from walls and will not be replaced for some time.*

Similarly at Invertay in 1897 there was

> *talk about closing the school for a time on account of a scarlatina epidemic disturbing the village. Fourteen cases in all can be traced to having a connection with the school.*

The hard pressed teacher at Kinnell, suffering very cramped conditions in 1875 before the building of a new school, complained that 'the noise caused by children coughing is very troublesome' and throughout the spring and early summer mentioned that whooping coughs and colds affected attendance. Even as late as the 1930s deaths among children from infectious diseases were not uncommon. The Stracathro log-book records that in December 1934 a pupil who had been at school only three days before died of scarlet fever while in the same school, in January 1935, the record states 'a third scholar has died from diphtheria'.

The length of time deemed necessary to recover from such illnesses is surprising to readers accustomed to present day medical procedures. At Braes of Coull in 1931 a little boy returned to school in March having been off with scarlet fever since the previous October. A boy who suffered from appendicitis in 1925 spent 12 weeks in Dundee Infirmary before returning to school. It was not until 1941 that head teachers recorded that immunisation against diphtheria had been offered to pupils and accepted in all cases. This proved too late for the Kilry pupil James Yule. The log-book records in October 1940 that

School reopened today under a deep sense of gloom. Word was received this morning that one of our most promising pupils had died of diphtheria contracted while he was on holiday,

The influenza epidemic of 1918 once again caused the closure of many rural schools in Angus since the Medical Officer of Health recommended closure for at least a fortnight where there were more than two cases in a school.

Little advice on health matters seems to have been provided prior to World War II but at Padanaram in 1921 the Band of Hope provided an address to senior pupils on 'the effects of alcohol on the heart'. However from the beginning of the twentieth century a real effort was made to ensure that rural children, often walking several miles to school, did have some hot food at lunch time in the winter months. The soup kitchen was an important part of school provision and various fund raising events were held to finance it. In February 1902 at Kinnell 'a magic lantern lecture entertainment was held in the school, the proceeds to the school soup kitchen' while at Carroch in 1912 'a concert was given this evening to raise money to put up a house for Soup Kitchen purposes' and five years later the school entertainment held in aid of 'The Hot Dinner Fund' raised nine pounds. There was a problem for school dinners at Stracathro in 1935 when 'a nest in the soup kitchen chimney delayed the cooking of the soup'. When meals were supplied from the depot at Forfar after 1945 there could still be problems. At Stracathro in 1947 'the dinner van stuck at Inchbare and the food containers had to be brought by sledge'.

From October 1946 several teachers note the provision of free school milk at the morning break each day. By the 1950s the travelling school dentist had become a feature of rural school life. Many rural children would normally not have visited the dentist and perhaps did not enjoy the experience as this extract from the Braes of Coull log-book for 1953 shows.

All children except one had stoppings or extractions and stoppings. School dismissed an hour early owing to extensive bleedings.

The Cleansing and Disinfecting of Schools

The following directions for the cleaning and keeping clean of schools have been prepared at the request of this Department by the expert advisors of the Local Government Board for Scotland and are issued under the joint authority of that Board and the Scotch Education Department. The directions are based upon actual experience, and take full account of practical difficulties. They represent the minimum precautions that ought to be enforced by every School Board who take due account of the health of the children attending their schools. The Department are, therefore, confident that these directions will receive the careful consideration of all School Boards and managers, and that, after a due interval, His Majesty's Inspectors will be able to report that, in every school in the country, the instructions now issued are being observed, except where it has happily been found possible to better them.

I. THE SOURCES OF DIRT IN SCHOOLS

The principal sources of dirt in schools are the following:— Shoes fouled by the dirt of the road and streets; clothing fouled by dust or dried organic secretions; scales shed from the skin of the body and scalp; dried organic secretions from the skin, mouth, nose; etc.; dust accumulating in hair and clothing; organic dust roused from floors by the movements of the children; cast hairs; woollen, linen, or cotton fibres; organic material blown from foul accumulations outside the school; soot and other inorganic dust particles.

The bodies of children are always in a state of very active growth. Hence the bodily secretions are relatively large in amount and readily become offensive in quality, even when the children are healthy. Within the school the children are continually moving. They keep the school dust in perpetual circulation; they add to the organic impurity of the atmosphere by respiration, by repeated coughing or sneezing, or, where slates are used, by spitting. Occasionally there are cases of skin diseases, such as itch (or scabies), or impetigo, or favus, or ringworm, or moist eczema. There are frequently "colds in the head," or inflamed eyes, or inflamed surfaces of the scalp, etc. These all contribute to the organic dust of a school. When infectious diseases—e.g., certain forms of inflamed eyes, or of inflamed throats or tonsils, scarlet fever, diphtheria, measles, whooping-cough, or chickenpox – are present, the dirt may become immediately dangerous as well as offensive. The particles of dust act as rafts to convey microbes of every sort from place to place.

The "close smell" so familiar in the schoolroom is due partly to the subtle organic impurities of the air breathed out by the children, partly to the decomposition of organic dirt on the children's bodies or in the room. Such decomposition is normally caused by microbes. Hence, to cleanse a schoolroom properly, it is necessary to destroy the germ-life as well as to remove the visible dirt. This is why periodic disinfection is advisable, even when no known infectious disease has been present.

31 *Rescobie School Soup Kitchen. In most schools the soup kitchen was often a small building behind the school*

Schools and Schoolhouses

Before 1872

By Acts of Parliament in 1633 and 1646 it was recommended to the several Presbyteries to see to the 'settling of schools in every landward parish' where children were to be taught reading, writing and the 'grounds' of religion. Parish schoolmasters were traditionally entitled to a house which very often incorporated the school. As far back as 1696 an Act of Parliament had laid down that 'the Heritors in every paroch meet and provide a commodious house for a school' which they defined a being not more than two rooms including the kitchen and with a garden of at least a quarter part of an acre. This ideal was never the case throughout Angus although some landlords did try to fulfil this obligation, and accommodation for the schoolmaster and his family was rarely 'commodious'.

However in their anxiety to provide a good education for their children, many local families were prepared to contribute towards school building. In St Vigeans in 1793 the schoolmaster's house is described as *'slated, consists of four rooms and two closets, and there is also a school-house of 38 feet long, lately built by contribution'.* Some scholars boarded in the schoolmaster's house and their fees together with his salary and other emoluments gave him an income of about £30 sterling a year. This was a good income for the time attractive to a well qualified dominie. At Carmyllie the OSA states:

> *Much praise is due to the people for promoting and encouraging the education of the youth of both sexes. They have subscribed a certain sum for building a school-house; and are determined to give every support to the person who is to have the charge of instructing the girls in different branches of needlework.*

In Glenesk the schoolmaster Alexander Ross had a small two-roomed house close to the loch. One room served as the home of the schoolmaster and his family. The other 12 foot room was the school. Later the school moved to Invermark and then Tarfside but it was not until 1873 that a new school and schoolhouse was provided by Lord Dalhousie. At the other end of the glen Waterside School was built in 1876 and remained open until 1965.

An Act of 1803 once again stipulated that the schoolhouse should be commodious but emphasised that it 'should not consist of more than two rooms including the kitchen'! A fenced garden of at least a quarter of a Scots acre and the use of 'fields for the ordinary purposes of agriculture and pasturage, as near and convenient to the school dwelling house as conveniently may be' should also be provided.

Interestingly, in the planned village of Letham, where George Dempster had encouraged the villagers to elect a representative body to act for them, the Feuers Committee felt confident enough by 1812 to make their own choice of schoolmaster rather than accept his recommendation. It was this committee which managed the first school, a single room built in the Den west of the Plash Mill with a dwelling house for the teacher attached. In 1829 the school was moved to the Hall in the Square but the tenants below the hall were not pleased to have a school meeting overhead and understandably applied for a reduction in rent.

32 *Letham Primary School was sympathetically extended*

At Aldbar in 1850 Patrick Chalmers could think of no finer tribute to his mother than the school he built in her memory. The substantial building has now been converted into an attractive house.

At Rescobie a new school was built in 1861 at a cost of £200. Details of the provisions for 85 pupils are of some interest:

Measurements providing 10 square feet of space for each child.:
length 29 feet
breadth 17 feet
height 12 feet

Cubic content 5916 cubic feet
Floor area 493 square feet

Soup kitchen (classroom)
length 24 feet
breadth 15 feet
area 360 square feet
accomodation for 36 pupils

Total accomodatiuon for 85 pupils

33 *Aldbar School, built by Patrick Chalmers, is now an attractive private house*

34 *Maryton School has been converted into a family home*

Schools and Schoolhouses after 1872

The 1872 (Scotland) Act obliged the newly established school boards to provide each headmaster with an adequate schoolhouse. In the ten year period after 1872 many fine stone built schools and school houses were built in Angus by the new school boards to replace the now totally inadequate accommodation. At Maryton the numbers increased so rapidly that a new school was imperative. Until the building was completed in 1878 the pupils worked in the church striving to write in the narrow pews. The teacher must have had an incredibly difficult few years and even in the first few months in the new school the pupils showed little improvement. However by the following year the visiting inspector commented on the remarkable improvement which had taken place.

The slate and paper work were done with accuracy on the whole, though the first and fourth standards are weak in Arithmetic, and the third standard should show a better knowledge of notation. But the general intelligence is at a very low ebb. The second standard and the upper division of the third standard, especially the latter, are tolerably smart. But the other classes above the second standard whether examined on the meaning of their Reading-books, the facts of History and Geography, the drift of Poem that some professed to have learned, showed a most utter stolidity. I cannot suppose that the intelligence of this district is naturally much worse than other country districts. The school has been several months in its new excellent premises and much better results will be expected. Some fair papers in History & Geography were shown, but the classes as a whole are weak in these subjects. Time seems to have been wasted in Physical Geography with no positive result. My Lords have ordered a deduction of one-tenth to be made from the Grant for faults of instruction in the upper standards (article 32 (b)). Mrs Marr is recognised as qualified under article 32 (C) 3.

Jms Denniston Corr

35 *Maryton School HMI Report 1878*

1879

April 4 The attendance slightly down this week, consequent on a few of the seniors having go to work out.

" Got my report from the Clerk this week. It is as follows.

Report

"The School has made a remarkable improvement, and is now in capital condition. The slate & paper work is particularly well done, there being hardly a failure in Arithmetic. The results are the more creditable considering the severe weather, and the prevalance of disease in the paris singing and sewing continue to be well taught"

David Marr Certificated Teacher Third Class — Mrs Marr, Teacher for the Industrial & Infant Departments. —

Correct

36 *Maryton School HMI Report 1879*

The problems were just as great at Kinnell. In November 1873 Mr Adamson, a joiner from Friockheim, measured the windows of the old school for 'the purpose of glazing'. Obviously some of the windows were lacking glass! Three days later the new school board members visited the school to decide what additional accomodation was needed. The following year a visiting inspector reported 'the school is now too crowded to be a pleasant place, either for the scholars or the teacher'. One problem was dealt with two years later when new toilets were erected 'at a distance from the school' but severe overcrowding still made the school an unpleasant place to be. The teacher was moved to write in the log-book in November 1877 that 'the atmosphere of the school was sickening and this acts as a great drag on the spirits of teacher and pupils'. Once again a sympathetic inspector reported:

With the narrow desks and crowded school no exercises on paper can be satisfactorily done. It is a marvel how anything like systematic teaching can go on in such premises when the school is so crowded.

The School Board had been active however. In April 1880 pupils at Kinnell were given an extended holiday for the demolition of the old school and the building of a fine new replacement. The headmaster's red sandstone house had a connecting door into the lofty ceilinged schoolrooms. With a garden and stable yard for the teacher and a large playing area and covered shed for the pupils it must have seemed a wonderful

37 *Kinnell School*

transformation. But such quality provision did not meet with the full approval of all ratepayers who were now obliged to pay the assessment decided upon by their local school board. In answer to many protests the Scotch Education Department, operating from London, sent a letter to the school boards advising restraint.

Many think that the school buildings are too grand and question the economy or morality of erecting on credit houses which are so expensive, stately and imposing. There are undoubtedly too many instances of school boards having been vastly too extravagant for the pockets of the poor ratepayers.

Some of the spacious, well-designed houses and schools of this period were so well constructed that they continue to offer desirable conversion into beautiful homes. The fine conversion at Kinnell for instance created a spacious wood-lined house of character, with care being taken to preserve where possible the original wooden doors.

Some School Boards did the absolute minimum in their school provision. Carroch School opened in 1875 but was so ill provided that in 1907 the Inspector's Report stated that 'The managers might surely after all these years get new desks and seats of proper construction.'

It took another two and a half years before the Board furnished half of the school with Dual Desks.

Even before many rural schools closed school houses in the years after World War II had ceased to be such an attraction for headmasters. Often the rooms seemed large and difficult to furnish with the smaller scale furniture which became popular in the 1950s and 60s. Old-fashioned bathrooms, once the height of luxury, now needed replacement. Nineteenth-century kitchens were not so desirable to the modern housewife. Perhaps the most important consideration was that new headteachers now saw a tied house as a liability. They felt they would be better off taking out a substantial mortgage on a private house and qualifying for tax relief. By the 1970s an increasing number of women were becoming headteachers in rural schools. Often they had family homes from which they had no desire to move. More and more school houses were surplus to requirements. At the time of local government reorganisation in Scotland after the Wheatley report the Angus education authority, like many others began to sell off these surplus schoolhouses.

a *Auchmithie School and schoolhouse have both become family homes*

b *The old schoolhouse at Kilry was almost derelict when Ian and Dorothy Cruikshank came into possession of it. They say, "We have tried to restore it sympathetically having no wish to alter the external aspect. We have added a small porch to the south aspect which covers the original entrance to the schoolhouse and also the lintel dated 1854"*

c *Lunan school and schoolhouse have been converted into two separate homes*

38 *Seven school conversions*

d *Farnell is now a gift shop and tea room. During the year seasonal fairs are held at House of Farnell*

e *David and Kathleen Page purchased Rescobie School and outbuildings in 1998. The dining hall and outside toilets were demolished. The photograph shows a rear view of the school and schoolhouse with Rescobie Loch in the background*

f *Logie Pert has been extensively refurbished*

g *The refurbished school and schoolhouse at Little Brechin*

School Memories

Mr Douglas, at the end of his career as schoolmaster at Ferryden in the middle of the nineteenth century remembered life in the village school:

The parents were very remiss in sending their children to school; and the children – the truants – when sent, behaved equally amiss in endeavouring to miss their way to school. The fees were on a very low scale, and the honesty of the payments equally low. My income was, therefore, very limited; and the irritation to which I was exposed, by irregular attendance and attempts to evade the payments for broken weeks, was enough to exhaust the patience of Job.

As to the capabilities of my pupils when fairly under my charge, I have no complaint to make. They showed an astonishing degree of cuteness, all circumstances considered. In reading they were not 'mim-mou'd', but shouted out in true stentorian style. Their writing showed no want of ink nor boldness of hand; but in arithmetic they often employed a system of logic which set all ordinary rules at defiance. For instance, on one occasion, an urchin had performed a calculation in Cloth Measure; and when told that the answer was half-a-yard too much he naively replied – 'Never mind, maister – look at that hole i' my breeks – it'll a'be needed.'

(DH Edwards, *Among the Fisher Folks of Usan and Ferryden*, p.156)

39 *Ferryden School children in the playground, 1905*

A Lunan pupil remembers school life in the early 20th century:

I left school in 1912. The roll then stood around 40. Families in those days were usually big and quite a few stayed in the parish for many years, which kept the school roll fairly steady.

Lunan School and Schoolhouse, Inverkelllor   Xmas /9.0

40 *Lunan School*

Our dominie, Archibald Wilson, taught at Lunan for more than 30 years and I look back on him with the greatest respect and admiration. I realise how much more he taught us than just our lessons, trying to instil the golden rule and much other good advice into our reluctant minds.

His wife was the finest woman I've ever known. Bonnie, capable and tireless in her efforts for any good cause and, in spite of much personal sorrow, was always cheerful, and willing to help and advise anyone at any time. She was the pivot on which our little community revolved and she kept in touch with old scholars long after they had grown up and left the parish.

We always had a school treat at New Year, the scholars submitting most of the programme. One year I remember my brother and the dominie's laddie were chosen to sing 'My Pretty Jane' as a duet. They were disgusted. 'Hearts of Oak' now or 'The British Grenadiers' that would have been something worth singing but cissy stuff like 'My Pretty Jane', Ach! They sang it just the same and made a good job of it too. Another classmate recited 'The Charge of the Light Brigade'. I can see him yet in the middle of the schoolroom floor, small of stature but full of vim and the joy of living, enacting the poem as he went along, with outstretched arm and clenched fist, "Cannon to right of them, cannon to left of them", he brought the house down.

We had a good Sunday school in those days too, our minister taking the older ones, his wife the wee ones, and our school missy the in-betweens. Our dominie played the kirk organ, and his wife led the praise, and what a lovely voice she had. When the schoolhouse family went on their annual summer holiday the kirk was dead without them. (*The People's Journal*, 1954)

Mr Frank Brown remembers Arrat School in the early years of the 20th century:

I started at the school when I was four. We had to walk two and a half miles. When there was snow my big brother used to carry me on his shoulders. I stayed at school for dinner. We got hot soup. We moved to Calcotts farm on the Brechin road when I was eight. I hated the teacher at Arrat School. I had come from Peterhead and he used to imitate my accent and make the others laugh. When I was eleven I got away from school for nearly three months! It was lambing time and I could help. A small hand could assist the sheep. I remember one day at lunch time we saw the Forfarshire Militia marching down the road from Brechin to Montrose. We boys just joined in the march, all the way to Montrose. We knew there would be trouble the next day at school but we didn't care.

Mrs Rachel Paton attended Inverkeilor School in the early 1920s:

My father worked at Redcastle farm so we had to walk nearly four miles to school. We always cut through the fields if it was dry. We had to be roaded by eight o'clock because you got the strap if you were late. I went with my brother and sisters, Anne, Dorothy and Alistair. There were five classes and the dominie, Mr Inglis, took the sixth. Miss Law had classes one and two. We just took a jeelie piece for our lunch and you got a drink of water if you were thirsty. Mind you in the winter we got hot soup. It was aye tattie soup. I didn't have any special uniform. I had a gym slip with a blouse in the summer and a jersey in the winter and we had a bonnet. When you got a new Sunday coat the old coat did for school. When we got home we got a piece but we had to wait 'til my father and mother were finished their tea 'til we got ours. My father came home at half past five and then my mother had to do the cows.

Mrs Christieson attended the primary classes at Inverkeilor School:

I walked two and a half miles to school. My father was a farmer and although he had a car we weren't given a lift. If the weather was bad we dried ourselves at the coal fire in the school room. We took sandwiches for lunch and in winter there was soup, always tattie soup! The farmer supplied potatoes and turnips and the butcher

41 *Pupils and staff at Inverkeilor school*

42 *Inverkeilor head teacher and staff. Miss Moir is seated*

supplied bones. *An old lady, Mrs Greig, who stayed in the village, came in every day to make the soup in the school boiler. The inspector used to come every year and we were told, "There's a gentleman coming to inspect you. Speak out loud because he's very deaf." I was terrified. The Brownies met in the school on a Saturday. When we came out one day Miss Kidd, my teacher, said, "We're going swimming in the bay." Mr Joss who was headmaster said, "Be very careful after the storm!" Six young women went. Two young ones were sunbathing and saw the other four swept out to sea. I never forgot that day!*

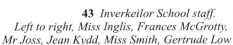

43 *Inverkeilor School staff.
Left to right, Miss Inglis, Frances McGrotty,
Mr Joss, Jean Kydd, Miss Smith, Gertrude Low*

Mr Jim Caithness attended Waterside School, Glenesk in the 1920s:

I started school in 1923 and stayed at Waterside until I was 14. It was a one teacher school with one large room with a schoolhouse at the far end. Another teacher came a half day a week to teach sewing to both the girls and the boys. I remember several teachers who worked in the glen until the school closed in 1965, because later on my wife and I acted as janitors. There was Miss Black, Mr Crowe, Miss Meldrum, Mrs Batchelor and finally Miss Dallachie. Mr Crowe lived at Tarfside and motor-cycled to school every day. He used to bring the bike into the school. He was well remembered because he used the cane. The school roll always fluctuated but the numbers were never very large. Some children from Holmhead crossed a bridge and walked about two and a half miles to school in all weathers. The children from Auchmull walked three and a half miles. For lunch you brought a 'piece in your pouch'. There was a coal fire, so water could be heated for tea. There was no shed, but two big beech trees provided shelter in the playground. The toilets were outside. Earlier, in the 1880s when my mother was at school in the glen she was taught in the Masonic Hall and had to bring a peat to school for the fire. Three generations of the Caithness family went to school at Waterside. My son Ron started school at three because several children at the school were off with chickenpox. His brother was the only one left in the class so Ron went with him. He had completed primary school work by the age of nine.

When I was janitor I had to deal with the coal fire but later there was a stove in the centre of the room. I used to sprinkle a brown dust called 'kill dust' on the wooden floor when it was swept. I remember that Daddy Thomson used to carry out tours up Glenesk with a machine and four horses. There were seats inside but some people sat on top. There was a man on the back with a tooter and when the machine passed the school the children all rushed up to wave. The war brought some changes for a short while. Evacuees came to the school from Dundee and an extra teacher came with them but many stayed only for a few days. Some Air Force officers were stationed at Invermark Lodge. They came down to visit the children. When they flew over the school on training flights the children waved to them. There was a Christmas-tree Party which took place at Tarfside and two taxis were provided to take the Waterside scholars. In the 1950s there was a visit to Edinburgh Zoo.

Jim Roberts attended Strathmartine School from 1922:

Our family lived in Bridgefoot village. My father was a signalman at Dundee West. The school was a modern building with some buildings still used from the old school. There were four classrooms. Pupils came from farm workers' families who moved regularly at term time and quarry workers' children as well as mill families.

There were three lady teachers and the dominie, Mr D.G. Dorward. One of the ladies, Miss MacCulloch, taught the Infants. The other two took the classes between Infants and Seniors. Mr Dorward had Seniors up to fourteen. The school had a drill hall and in part of the old school cookery and joinery rooms. The land round the school belonged to Jeffrey Cox, a Dundee Jute merchant. My father was a friend of his gamekeeper, Tom Cuthill, who was an international clay-pigeon shot. The poachers found that he was also a quarter-miler when he chased them from the land!

The three lady teachers came by train in the morning but after school had to walk a mile to Downfield at night to get a train. I remember Miss Lyle was my teacher, and some afternoons a friend of my brother would make her livid. He was Chalmers the butcher's delivery boy and had Wednesday afternoon off. Sitting on the school wall, he would see me in the class and would wave. This seemed to annoy her.

Not far from the school on the Dighty Burn was a bone-meal mill owned by the Rodger family. The ladies of the family ran a Sunday School. About half of our school went. I still have the little book, the Shorter Catechism, and remember the Christmas treat and the summer picnic. Their brother Johnny sometimes let us have rides on his wooden model railway. I left Strathmartine for Morgan Academy when I was 12.

THE SHORTER CATECHISM.

Question 1. What is the chief end of man?

Answer. Man's chief end is to glorify God, and to enjoy Him for ever.

Q. 2. What rule hath God given to direct us how we may glorify and enjoy Him?

A. The word of God, which is contained in the Scriptures of the Old and New Testaments, is the only rule to direct us how we may glorify and enjoy Him.

Q. 3. What do the Scriptures principally teach?

A. The Scriptures principally teach what man is to believe concerning God, and what duty God requires of man.

Q. 4. What is God?

A. God is a Spirit, infinite, eternal. and unchangeable in His being, wisdom, power, holiness, justice, goodness, and truth.

Q. 5. Are there more Gods than one?

A. There is but one only, the living and true God.

44 *The Shorter Catechism which Jim Roberts had as a boy at Strathmartine School in the 1920s*

William Thomson attended Hillside School in the 1920s:

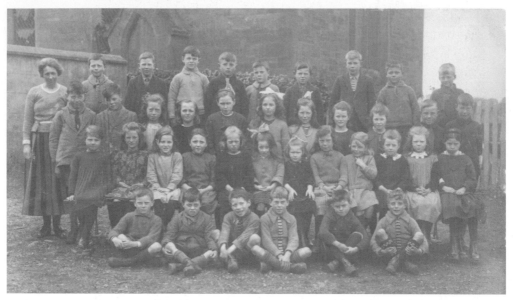

45 *William Thomson attended Hillside School in the 1920s. Miss Grieve is the teacher in the photograph. William is in the back row two along from Miss Grieve. William and his brother David (third from right in back row) moved with their mother to his grandfather's farm at Midgrip when his father, a Cameron Highlander, was killed in World War I*

Mrs E Eadie has memories of her schooldays at Kettins in the early 1920s:

When I was at Kettins School the school had three classrooms and three teachers so each teacher taught more than one class. The teachers then were Mr Andrew, the headmaster, Miss Reid and Miss Robertson, the very well-liked infant teacher. She cycled daily from Coupar Angus, but later bought a car to use. She was also, at one time, Lady Provost of Coupar Angus, possibly the first lady provost in her own right in Scotland.

There was a school garden and Mr Andrew was in charge. Only the senior pupils were involved. It was laid out in vegetable plots – each plot had a team with a leader. There was also a team in charge of the War Memorial and shrubbery area. Several afternoons in the summer we spent weeding, raking etc. and just before the summer holidays Mr Andrew inspected the work and prizes were given to the best team – a 6d. or 3d. (old money). By the way, there is a little bird buried in a corner of the shrubbery which was given a 'proper' funeral by two or three of us as we sang 'Safe in the arms of Jesus' over the grave! I presume the janitor looked after the garden when pupils weren't there, and that things like potatoes and turnips would be stored for use in the soup which was made for the pupils in the winter.

I have other memories too, like the football field (now built on) and strictly boys' territory except when the girls had their annual French cricket match. Then there

KETTINS SCHOOL GARDEN - HORTICULTURAL SECTION.

KETTINS SCHOOL GARDEN ROCKERY.

KETTINS WAR MEMORIAL AND ENTRANCE TO SCHOOL GARDENS.

46
Mr Andrews, the head teacher of Kettins School, pioneered the use of school gardens and school meteorological stations

*was the annual picnic to Hallyburton, where I was congratulated by the laird –
Mr Graham Menzies for jumping the highest in the sports. I overlooked the fact he
was congratulating the wrong girl! Mrs Menzies visited the school each year to
judge the girls' sewing work, and donated a prize. I was lucky enough to be the
winner one year and was given a lovely silver bar brooch with a blue stone in it.*

*The infant and junior classrooms were divided by a partition which could be
concertina'd back to make a fair-sized hall for concerts or dances. There was
something called Slipperene which was sprinkled on the floor to make it easier to
dance on. Failing Slipperene, Lux Flakes were used! The last year I was there the
headmaster's room was divided into two, and the new room was used for visiting
science and cookery teachers. I wonder, does the bell still ring from the roof?
It was like a church bell and its sound carried a long way to warn us laggard country
pupils to hurry up.*

Bill Beedie started at Carmyllie West School in 1928

*I started school in 1928. The school jotters were labelled Forfarshire Education
Committee rather than Angus. I usually walked the one and three quarter miles to
school over a mostly cart road although I later cycled. In the summer when the grass
was dry and you could walk over the fields, it was just a little over a mile. In the
1930s, Scotland, or Angus or Carmyllie at least, had a plague of rabbits. On my
way to school along the edge of the fields I would set a few snares and check them
on my way home. My pocket money came from selling my few rabbits at 3d. each
to the butcher, whose van called twice a week. Though snares were not illegal then,
on reflection I'm not proud of my enterprise. However it was no more inhumane
than the myxomatosis introduced later from Australia as a nationwide cure for the
problem.*

*There were eight classes for pupils aged from 5 to 14 but I think the 13- to 14-year
olds may have made one class. We sat in pairs at wooden desks with a slot at the
front to take our slates and a channel to take our slate pencil or pen and a hole to
take an inkwell. Most writing was done on the slate in the junior classes but we
also had jotters and copy-books used specifically in writing lessons with metal
nibbed pens that were dipped in ink-wells. Desk tops lifted up to give a cavity
wherein we stored pens, pencils, rubbers, jotters and a little tin with a damp sponge
or cloth to wipe our slates. Desks were arranged in rows, one row to a class,
so that you looked at the shoulders of the pair in front. The clever ones were at the
back and the dunderheads at the front next to the teacher.*

*The total roll was 50 or 80. For some time we only had two teachers, the dominie
and one lady teacher. Then we had a third and the big room was partitioned into
two. Each teacher had three or four classes in the same room. In my last year in*

47 *Pupils at Carmyllie West School in 1933. Bill Beedie is in the front row, second from left*

the dominie's room, the lady teacher, Miss Gray, gave me piano lessons once a week after school.

My first infant teacher, Miss Imrie, married Dave Hume, the farmer at Mains of Carmyllie, and we all got a bag of sweeties from the bride. Her replacement, Mrs Smart, a more mature lady, was well liked and respected and was still there when I left. The dominie throughout my time there was Harry L Officer, who I believe served in the army in World War I, though he seldom spoke of it. Harry had many friends in the district, was well respected and entered fully into the infrequent community activities. In school I remember him as a fairly strict disciplinarian though, to be fair, it was a pleasure to be in his classroom most of the time. Most fine days after his lunch he would join the big boys' football game in the playground for 10 or 15 minutes before blowing the whistle for afternoon classes. I personally was very grateful to him for some extra evening tuition prior to the bursary exam which gave me a season-ticket on the bus for three year's secondary education.

No particular textbooks stand out in my memory, but I do remember one in the junior classroom with stories about 'The Boy who Cried Wolf'; 'The Pied Piper of Hamelyn' and the Chinese chap who accidentally discovered roast pork. Later, in the dominie's room, we seemed to write lots of compositions, which I hated. We had an annual school picnic and went by coach to the beach at Carnoustie.

Nobody swam but we all paddled in the sea and queued up for ice cream and to slide down the chute, which was quite a novelty for country bairns! I don't remember a school party but we did have Sunday school parties in the manse at Christmas. School concerts were infrequent, but I do remember dressing up as a prince for a play once. The dominie organised some good evening concerts in the school by collecting local adult and juvenile talent for sketches, vocal and instrumental turns. I remember going back to school one evening in 1936, after I'd gone to Forfar Academy, to hear the abdication speech by King Edward VIII on a wireless set Mr Officer had erected in school for the public to come and hear. Not a lot of country-folk had radios in these days.

48 *Bill's acting debut as a prince in a school concert*

In the boys' and girls' playgrounds the sheds were open on one side and had one long wooden seat. They doubled as shelter and bicycle shed but there were surprisingly few bicycles. There were no toilets inside the school building and those outside were of the thunderbox variety. As far as games went, the unsuccessful attempts to 'guddle' trout in the local burn were soon abandoned. The boys occasionally played rounders and there was a game with a prepared piece of wood of square section (one and a half inches by one and a half inches) about 6 inches long whittled to a point at each end and numbers 1 to 4 cut in the four sides. I think we called it a 'cattie'. We each had a stick about 2 feet long and, in turn, hit the pointed end of the cattie to make it jump and while it was in the air we tried to hit it away from base. The number showing upwards when it landed was the number of hits we each could have. The farthest from base after your 'go' was the winner. The older boys played football in the playground most lunch times. Windows got broken, but I remember no punishments for the dominie was usually playing too! About 1930 or so we all stood in the playground looking towards Arbroath and watched the Graf Zepplin floating down the east coast. One day an unfortunate game of 'tig' ended with Dave Melville spending a week or two in Arbroath Infirmary when he ran out of the playground gate into the path of a moving car. Very soon we had a rail erected across the gate.

For school meals we had a soup kitchen during the winter months. I think we paid a halfpence a day. Mae Milne made the soup in a large cast-iron coal- or wood-fired boiler built into the corner of the soup kitchen. We queued up and soup was ladled into white enamelled bowls which we carried to tables in the bigger room. Some carried a piece of bread to eat with their soup. I don't think anyone declined Mae's soup. We were all glad of it. In the summer the soup kitchen was closed and Mae Milne undertook casual farm work such as planting potatoes, picking strawberries, gathering spuds or spreading dung, along with her school cleaning work. Then we carried a 'piece', often bread and cheese or just bread and jam. In good weather we would sit and eat on the playground wall or on the doorsteps. In wet weather the sheds were used or we could stay in our classroom.

I left the district early in 1939 due to family circumstances and joined the RAF later that year, aged 16. On visiting Carmyllie many years later, I found the farms had got much bigger and highly mechanised; the crofts like our one had mostly disappeared and the West School had closed in 1970. Last time I passed the school was partly a large store and partly a dwelling house while the Free Kirk was a tattie shed. In retrospect I probably enjoyed most at school the opportunity to meet and play with people of my own age. Though I was fortunate in having a brother, rural dwellings were usually fairly isolated.

Mrs Cooper began her schooldays at Westerton School, Rossie in the 1930s:

I lived at Rossie Moor so it was a fair walk to school, three miles there and back every day, rain or shine, first across a field, then across the moor and then two more fields. My sister who is sitting next to me in the picture was barely four when she started but she was never off a single day until she left school ten years later. The teacher liked us all to bring a clean hanky and my wee sister used to have hers tied on the belt of her frock so that she wouldn't lose it.

The school had two rooms and when I was there we had 17 boys and 8 girls in the class. There were no school kitchens. We all took a play-piece and something for our dinner and the afternoon playtime. My mother had hens so we always had eggs or a piece of chicken for our piece. I took four slices of bread, one for the morning, two at dinner time and one for later. I always had a drink or soup in a flask. There were four dry toilets, two for the boys and two for the girls in a shed in the playground. It was always kept very clean.

49 *The children at Westerton School. Mrs Cooper and her sister are in the second row*

Our teacher was Mrs Dewar, a widow, and she was good but firm. She had complete control. No one ever spoke back. When someone misbehaved they were sent out to weed the garden. You had to lay out the long roots of Bishop Weed on the path to show you had pulled it all up. Everybody hated that! We used slates at school. We were supposed to have a rag to wipe the slate, but a lot of the boys used to spit on it and rub it with their cuffs. Every three weeks the slates were scrubbed in the wee sink. Sometimes the inspector came and he always stood at the fire leaning on the guard and one time he burned his backside!

We played lots of games like 'Kick the Can', 'Middle' (a bit like 'Hide and Seek') and skipping games. We used to tie the rope on a post in the teacher's garden. We could easily amuse ourselves, for country bairns didn't look for big things. The school picnic was a great day. Westerton School and Rossie School went together one year to Dunninald Mains. Another year we went to Lunan. We set off with two horses and carts and had an afternoon picnic with Craig School. We sat on straw on the carts and two pipers played tunes all the way. I remember the farmer had lent a big cart-horse one year and it was decorated with bells and ribbons on the harness.

I remember the day Princess Margaret was born at Glamis in the month of August because there was terrible thunder and lightning. We were all a bit frightened because of the noise but the teacher sat down at the piano and played very loudly

74

50 *Children of the former Craig School in the 1930s. Miss Cuthbert is the teacher. Jim Mearns is standing next to her and his brother David is also in the back row 4th from right*

and we all sang songs like 'Horsey, Horsey keep your tail up'! When the thunder stopped, Mrs Dewar said, "Now go home immediately. Don't stop on the way."

One thing I hated at school was that I had to wear glasses. I was the only bairn who had them and sometimes I didn't wear them because the others made fun of me. One day I forgot them and Mrs Dewar said, "I will make sure you never forget them again." She sent me the three miles home to get them so I had to walk an extra six miles that day! I hated the glasses so much that one time, when we were on a train, I threw the glasses out of the window and said the wind did it. But I got another pair. There was a wee girl at the school who used to say she was a gift from God. Her mother was housekeeper at the big hoose and so she always had a bar of toffee or an apple with her. She used to give me a bite of her apple if I let her walk up and doon at playtime with the glasses. Then I'd grab them off her face when the bell rang.

We had quite a lot to do with Rossie Farm School when I was there, and the wife of the headteacher at Rossie, Mrs Carson, always gave a prize to the sewing class of an embossed silver thimble. We always called her 'Auld Kirsty' behind her back but she was a nice woman. Anyway I won the thimble one year and the next year I won it again. The second prize was a workbox and I asked the girl who won it if she would change with me. Not Her! But it worked out fine in the end because

I had two lasses and I was able to give them both a silver thimble. Years later I met the girl with the workbox and she said it had fallen apart!

I married a soldier in the regular army and the regiment went to Penang, India. I was very upset when my first bairn died. I looked at all the native children who did not seem to have anyone caring for them and I thought, "Why did my bairn die and they're all right?" But after a while I began to think I could help them. The regiment had a sewing machine and I got a loan of it. I made trousers and wee dresses for some of the children and soon they began coming every day. I remembered my schooldays at Westerton and I used to do the things I did then. Folks at home sent out the Sunday Post, The People's Friend, The Beano *and* The Dandy *and the children loved the pictures and I played the games we used to play. So my school days came in handy far away from home.*

Miss Dorothy Meldrum began her training as a teacher of domestic science in the 1920s:

51 *Miss Meldrum in 2003*

In 1922 I went to Aberdeen College in King Street to follow the three-year course of training. My first post was at Arbroath High school in 1925. Some of my pupils came from the fishing communities of Angus. I remember one day the girls were very excited because they had got their fish-wives' uniform, navy skirt, blouse and shawl. They left school at fourteen and began delivering fish. These same girls were allowed to leave their desks to look out at the Queen's train passing on one memorable occasion, but they only saw the roof!

Mrs J Hill, Mrs Sheila Lindsay and Mrs E Burnett remember their schooldays at Guthrie in the 1930s:

The teachers at Guthrie at that time were Mr Thomson (nicknamed Hattie), Mrs Mitchell and Miss Gibb. Mrs Hall recalls, "We used slates for everyday work with jotters for writing once a week. In winter we had a lovely big fire in the classroom which was especially appreciated when we had walked through the deep snow to school from home."

Mrs Burnett remembered, "There was a soup kitchen at Guthrie where Miss Niven, helped by the senior girls, made soup in winter time." Mrs Lindsay recalls, "The soup was served in white enamel buckets by older pupils. Our bowls were white enamel with a dark blue rim round the top. Afterwards we helped wash up and were rewarded with superb – tasting Swiss milk Tablet also made by Mabel Niven."

In the 1950s, Mrs Betty Carcary was also a pupil at Guthrie. "When I was at school the subject I remember as my favourite lesson was History. In the playground we played skipping and rounders, hopscotch and tig. In the headmaster's garden the boys cut the grass while the girls weeded. My schooldays were the best years of my life."

Mr Ed Cuthbert went to school at Hillside in 1930 and later attended Maryton and Inverkeilor:

I walked from Stone o' Morphie to Hillside when I was five. The wee ones got out at three o'clock in the afternoon and then I waited until four for the bigger ones to get out. Mr George Bruce Williams was the headmaster. We all hud to bring our own duster and a perfume bottle with water. We kept the slates in a slot in the desk and if your writing was good enough you got a jotter.

I left Hillside when I was eight to go to Maryton. It was a two-teacher school. Miss Nichol lived in the school house, and I remember her car registration was BSR 276. I won the dux medal at Maryton. When I was eleven or twelve, I went to Inverkeilor on a service-bus from Denhead. It was 6d. a day. The boys held the girls back so they would miss the bus and often we ran to the next stop so that we only paid 4d. Then we could get five Woodbines out of the cigarette machines at the shop for 2d. The soup for school lunch was made in a boiler and brought into the room in steel buckets. It cost one penny a day and if there were three children in a family the third was free. Mr Carrick was head teacher. He always kept his belt on the table. We had a gardening class with a prize for the boy with the best plot. Our drill was held outside in the playground.

Ed completed his schooling at Inverkeilor winning prizes. He remembers his Edinburgh/Angus Club prize. Few of his contemporaries were able to go on to Montrose Academy, then fee-paying, because of cost.

County of Angus. Education Committee.

Maryton SCHOOL,

Class, *Adv 1st Year*

Dux PRIZE

Awarded to

Edward Cuthbert

for General Excellence & Progress

Wm Nicoll Head Teacher

June 1937

52 *Ed Cuthbert was Dux of Maryton School in 1938*

Mrs Mary Cuthbert went to school at St Cyrus:

I lived with my sister at my grand-mother's house in St Cyrus when my brother was to be born. We went to St Cyrus school at the beginning of the war and I remember going downstairs to the shelters carrying my gas mask for air-raid drill.

One of the things I recall about school was the connection with the Forsyth-Grants from Ecclesgreig Castle. I broke my leg when I was at school and lay for six weeks, and Gladys Forsyth-Grant came to our house to give me physiotherapy. On another occasion, names were pulled out of a hat at the Brownies to see who could

53 *Attendance certificate*

go to the castle to see the wedding presents and bride's dress, when Fenella married Air Marshall Fogarty.

In summer the whole school went by train from St Cyrus to Monifieth for an outing, with a picnic provided by the baker. A lasting memory of 'mental' arithmetic at school is of children having hair pulled by the teacher or fingers smacked with a ruler if they made a mistake.

Jim Wallace attended Chapelton School from 1939 and still lives in the village today

He describes the village during his school days:

Chapelton was a small village between Inverkeilor and Friockheim consisting of John Soutar's joinery at the crossroads, auld Jock Neil's shoppie selling sweets and lemonade, the smithy of Geordie Jarrett and brother Ed, and the shepherd's house, Annie, Jim and David Buicks. Then there was the school. When I went there the teachers were the Misses McNiven. They retired and Miss Pearson was head Missie and Miss Robertson was junior Missie. I stayed a mile away at Millfield and had to walk every day, rain or shine, with the children from Waulkmill up the Low Road, or Leckie as it was known. World War II broke out just after I started school. I was in the wee room with Miss McNiven's class. We were issued with gas-masks one of which I still have. As the war meant everything had to be saved, the older ones used to get a loan of John Soutar's hand-cart and go round collecting cardboard and waste paper. This meant a good eight-mile walk once a month on Friday afternoon. I remember V.E. Day. When I came home from school my mother had the flags out.

I remember we got Horlicks at piecie time. I never ever tasted Horlicks like it! At denner time in winter we wid get soup made by Auld Stottie who was a wee wifie aye dressed in black with a peenie. She made bra soup as the farmers wid hand in tatties, neeps and the like. Jock Ross the gamie wid hand in rabbits, hares, pigeon, pheasants. Auld Stottie stayed next door to Davie Buick. His house was next the village hall and dancing lessons were taught, before my time, by Dancie Williamson who had a widden leg!

When I went into the big room at school I graduated to doing the Missie's garden. I enjoyed it but it didn't do my schooling any good. I can tell you the teachers stood no nonsense and everyone had to behave and salute the teacher, Bobby policeman and the minister, if seen after school hours. At the prize-giving we had to do a play about Rule Britannia and sing it. We did at the end of the war get a school picnic and went to Montrose Beach. It was a cauld day! After the Tattie Holiday the kids would get new breeks and a thick blue jersey and blue heavy coat. By next summer they were in holes including the boots and socks.

I did enjoy my school days. Summer seemed to be always nice and warm. In the country we really lived very well. We had hens for eggs and to eat. We grew our own vegetables and tatties and had our own cows for milk. My mother made butter and cheese and we got curds and whey in summer. There was honey from bees and home-made bread. We killed a pig once a year. So did neighbours, so meat was exchanged. We got extra petrol for the tractor so it was also used in the van. So one night we set off to Arbroath to the pictures with a young pig in the back. We left the van and the pig at Culloden farm.

When I left Chapelton I went on to Arbroath High School. I had to work very hard and left in 1949 with 75% marks.

Miss Jolly's first teaching appointments were in rural schools:

I started teaching in 1936 in Menmuir. In 1939, just before the war, the headmaster had to give returns for accommodation for evacuees. I had to walk all round the area. It was a complete revelation to me to see the 'hovels' people were living in, with dirt floors and little furniture. My next teaching appointment was at Craigo School. Mr Morris was headmaster. Miss Rita Mortimer and I were the teachers. At that time the MacPherson Grants lived in Craigo House. Mrs MacPherson Grant came to school to present the prizes at the end of term. The pupils came from farms and from mill workers' families. The water bailiff's children came to Craigo School as did children from Logie village. Pupils could stay at Craigo until 15.

I lived in digs when I was teaching at Menmuir but was able to live at home when I moved to Craigo. The Montrose to Laurencekirk train stopped at Craigo station.

During the war we had gas-mask rehearsals in the morning. There were no air-raid shelters at Craigo. The children were supposed to get under their desks if there was an air-raid warning. There was one Glasgow evacuee came to school. When the infants got out of school at 3pm and ran across the road the child, staying in Craigo to be safe from the war, was killed by a lorry. After that the head teacher saw them over the road for a wee while.

54 *On the day Craigo School closed in 2000 the pupils wrote their names on the shed wall*

Mrs Christieson started her teaching career at Logie Pert School in 1942:

I did my teacher-training at Dundee. The College specialised in training for rural schools' teaching. Students came from other country areas such as the Borders. We stayed in a hostel. When the hostel was needed for wartime accommodation we stayed in digs.

There were two teachers at Logie Pert when I started. The headmaster was in the services. Miss Jessie Stott was Headmistress and taught primaries 5, 6 and 7 and the pupils in the senior section where they stayed till age 14. I taught primaries 1,2,3 and 4. There was a big central partition which divided the large schoolroom and could be moved when the school was used for dances and whist-drives etc. After two year's teaching, I gained my 'Parchment' as the qualification was called.

Many Logie Pert pupils had never been to town. The school took them for their first trip to Montrose and the beach. The pupils came from farms mostly, but sometimes travellers' children came to school. One parent objected to this and complained about her child sitting beside a traveller's child. I wrote back pointing out that these children were cleaner than 50% of the others!

When I taught infants, Montessori blocks were introduced for the teaching of arithmetic. Some teachers consigned them to the cupboard saying, "They've got two hands with fingers and they've always got them with them." There was very little equipment in the school when I started so I made number cards in my own time to help the children.

Mrs Pam Cranswick attended Lundie School where her father was headmaster:

Mr Moyes, Pam's father, became headmaster at Lundie in 1939 just before the start of World War II. All teachers over 30 were exempt from the call-up so he remained there all during the war years. Pam remembers

55 *Mrs TP Douglas Murray opening the Muirhead School Sale of work. Mr Moyes, the schoolmaster, and Mr JP Hastie are also present*

There were two rooms in Lundie School and Frances Stewart taught the first four classes in the wee room and my father taught Primary 5, 6 and 7 in the big room. My father was always referred to as the dominie. The school had a stove for heating and the teacher kept the stove going from the scuttle of anthracite. The milk for the children was delivered in a flagon. In winter it was sent over to our house and my mother made cocoa for break-time. For school dinners we trooped up to the hall for soup and bread. In summer we had sports in a farmer's field. The school children and the whole village went on a double-decker bus to Arbroath for a picnic. Some children had never been there before. At lunchtime the Co-op van came with an urn of tea and 'baggies'. In the afternoon there was shopping or swimming at the pool.

Archie Briggs who lived in the house at Lundie castle often provided food for picnics and presents for the Christmas party.

My father later became headmaster at Muirhead of Liff. The school trip to London for the Festival of Britain in 1952 was a wonderful experience for the pupils.

56 *Muirhead of Liff pupils in London*

Mrs Frances Stewart joined Kilry School in December 1943. She enjoyed telling the present-day pupils how things had changed:

Living at Scruschloch, I had to walk three miles to and from school every day, via 'Loanhead'. There were no taxis or lifts in those days. If it was very wet, my father would pick us up but mostly we walked. We left home at 7.30am each morning and it was after 5pm when we arrived home.

Miss Johnstone, who lived in the schoolhouse, was headmistress and Miss Ross, who lived in Alyth, was the assistant. Two rooms were in use, with a partition between, no lovely carpets, just wooden floors. On very cold mornings we were given a cup of cocoa when we arrived at school. The kettle was boiled on the stove which heated the classroom. Before lessons each morning we said 'The Lord's Prayer'. We had big wooden desks with an inkwell in the corner. The lid of the desk opened up to store our books and slates, which were in constant use due to a shortage of paper during the war. At morning break we had little bottles of milk, which were delivered by Mr Hunter of Auchrannie farm. Sometimes the milk would be frozen and had to be thawed out beside the stove. Miss Hunt who lived in the cottage across from the school made and served soup in the soup-kitchen. Latterly we had school dinners which came from Forfar every day in big urns to keep them warm. Toilets were at the opposite end of the playground from the school, girls on one side of the shelter and boys on the other.

As it was wartime we had to carry our gas-masks to school with us every day. Once a week we had a practice to see how quickly we could get our gas-masks on, in case we were bombed with gas. Quite often in the winter we were off school because of snow, as the farms didn't have big tractors and diggers like they have now. The roads were cleared manually which took a long time and a lot of very hard work. Miss Johnstone always made sure we had plenty homework to keep us busy and so we wouldn't fall too far behind the others in the class.

In the summer the class and the teacher went on a ramble beside the burn to collect rosehips for rosehip syrup. Each school was awarded a prize depending on how many rosehips were picked.

Towards the end of the war all the children and their mothers were taken on an outing to Monifieth by bus. It was a great event. After races and games on the sands we were each given a bag of sandwiches and a cup of tea – no Coke or juice! When war ended, all the school children dressed in fancy dress and joined in a parade round Kilry. I was a pack of cards and my brother was Oor Wullie. The parents and older people had parties and dances in the Hall. Class was dismissed at ten to four in the afternoon.

57 *Kilry School today*

Tom Frost delivered bakery products to the rural schools around Angus in the 1940s:

I remember delivering to Inverkeilor, Lunan, Westerton of Rossie, Maryton, Rossie, Dun and out to St Cyrus among others. As well as the school house order the children usually had a halfpenny for their roll. At Westerton, where there were about 20 children, Miss Kinnear would let the children out to the van even if it wasn't playtime. Most didn't buy a roll and wanted a fancier bun etc. At lunch time a boiler of soup was made for the children. They came to Westerton from West Mains of Rossie, Mountboy farm, other farms on the Gighty burn and the children of staff at Rossie School.

One day when I was delivering at Rossie itself a young man in Air Force uniform gave me ten shillings saying, "Give the boys anything they want." He had been a pupil at Rossie before 1936. A Glasgow boy who was there around this time found it a big change, He announced, "Aye, they're trying to make us into farmers. No me. When I get oot o' here I'll get my milk oot a bottle, no a coo!"

Lunan was a two-class school with the schoolhouse attached. The teacher lived there with her mother. I delivered to the schoolhouse and if I arrived when it wasn't playtime the children didn't get out to the van. The pupils came from the village and the surrounding farms like Drumbertnot, Courthill, Arbikie. There were always children from the Brown and Leal families at Lunan. Miss Jessie Stott who was a teacher there came out from Montrose on the train to Lunan station. I remember the snow being so bad I couldn't get up the road to Westerton after getting up Rossie Braes. I was frozen serving while the farmers came down in horses and carts and on tractors.

Another teacher I remember was the head teacher from Ferryden. He regularly cycled over to Montrose golf course with his clubs over his shoulder and his wee terrier running beside him and then round the course.

Margaret Alexander's Memories of Lunan School in the Second World War:

I remember the Polish soldiers living next door in the school house. There were concerts in the large school room with the smaller pupils perched on the high window sills. I remember picnics to the bay. I lived opposite the school in a crofter's cottage and my mother made the school soup from a sheep's head. She used a boiler in a small outhouse in the playground. Then the soup was served to the children in the schoolroom.

Mr John Riddell had his primary education at Maryton School:

I started school after the Easter holidays. I had to walk about a mile to school. There were two class rooms with a coal stove in each room and between 40 and 50 pupils. I remember two teachers, Miss Nichol and Miss Scott. Miss Nichol, the head teacher, retired in 1950. Then we had Mr James Smith. He had been wounded in the war. His wife was a nurse. He often left the class to go to the school house to have his wounds dressed.

I walked from Forfar junction to Maryton School. If it was a rainy day Miss Scott used to stop for me in her Morris 12 car. As we came near Maryton Church

58 *John Riddell*

I would slide down in the seat so I wouldn't be seen in the teacher's car by my friends. I would be called the teacher's pet. Miss Scott used to say, "Sit up Johnny!"

I do not remember any special textbooks except a reading book. I enjoyed craft work. I remember spending months making a coronation coach and horses. We went on summer picnics to Kirriemuir one year and another time to Newport on the 'Fifie', the ferry from Dundee. At our Christmas parties local people made the food, like dumpling.

The boys and girls had separate playgrounds. There was a shed in the playground and outside toilets. We used to play rounders and football and sliding on the ice in winter. When we were in the top primary class we had to weed the schoolhouse garden. There was a flat-roofed dinner hall separate from the school. Scott the carrier brought the school lunches on a covered lorry from Montrose. We had school milk. I usually had bread and jam or syrup for playtime.

59 *John Riddell's class in the 1950s with Miss Christie and Mr Smith*

60 *Evelyn Mouat with her class in Inverkeilor in the 1950s*

Mrs Evelyn Mouat began teaching at Inverkeilor in 1952:

There were four teachers in the Primary Department at that time and I taught Primary 4 and 5 in a small brick building which had two classrooms. It was separate from the main building. There were less than 30 pupils in my class. One of the primary teachers was Miss Gertie Low who was a notable character and liked by all. Mr Ramsay, the head teacher, was a very strict disciplinarian with the tawse being the ultimate sanction. It was seldom used in the classroom as the country children were usually well-behaved. Mr James Bruce, who was the technical teacher in the Junior Secondary Department, taught gardening to the senior boys in the school garden.

61 *Ferryden School as it is today*

Mr Tom Long came as Head Teacher to the school at Ferryden in 1961:

I went to the school on the understanding that a new school was to be built. When I was asked what I would like the building to look like, one of the suggestions I made was that the entrance should look like a hotel. It should have a reception area with paintings on the walls instead of children's work, but there would be designated areas and a showcase for pupils' work. Over my years as a teacher after the war, I saw many changes in attitudes to teaching. Learning by understanding came in to vogue. Music, art and woodwork were thought of as 'frills', but they should have been an integral part of the curriculum. I seldom used the belt following advice I had been given that its use should be 'seldom but memorable'.

Mrs Ann Duncan attended Kingsmuir School from 1964 to 1968:

I started Kingsmuir School in Primary 1 and left at the end of Primary 5. I didn't have a 'first day' at school as I was the Dominie's daughter. The Missie – Mrs Patullo – was absent from work as her husband was unwell, and my mother was the only person available on supply. Despite having myself aged four, my sister aged two and a new baby brother to care for, she took over primaries 1, 2 and 3 on a temporary basis – with pre-schoolers in tow. I remember the high pram at the front of the classroom and my sister enjoying free play. I was set to work with the Primary 1 pupils and when Mrs Patullo returned it was decided that I had settled in well and would continue at school. The schoolhouse was across the road from the school and an early memory is of being carried, screaming, back to school after lunch. I wanted to watch 'The Wooden Tops' but as a school pupil no longer had that option. Perhaps I hadn't settled in completely!

The school had two rooms – the 'big' or 'dominie's' room and the 'wee' or 'missie's' room. Primaries 1–3 were in the 'wee' room, 4–6 in the room next door. Each room had a stove with a metal guard around it. This was festooned with dripping gloves in winter and crates of frozen milk gently thawed on the hearth. At the end of the summer term my father used one stove to burn all the old papers and rubbish before closing the school. The classroom had three areas of desks clearly marking progression from class to class. Primary 3 sat nearest a 'beautiful' chart of cursive letters. I knew that when I reached Primary 3, I would at last be able to write properly, just like the chart! The windows were too high to see out, but I spent many a happy hour watching 'fairies' – dust particles dancing in the sunshine. Beside the Primary 1 desks was a wall-cupboard which housed 'treats' like beads to thread and peg boards with which to create patterns. Each desk had a lifting lid and contained a chalk board, a rag duster, a tobacco tin of plasticine and a box of 'Cuisenaire rods'. Jotters and textbooks were also kept in the desk.

Each morning started in the same way. We said a 'prayer':

"Good morning," said the shining sun,
"A happy day to you!"
"Good morning," said the little birds,
"The sky is nice and blue!" Etc.

On Mondays dinner monies were paid, and on Tuesdays the school savings money was collected to be invested for the future in the Trustees Savings Bank. For summer holidays we were given a strip of six envelopes to fill weekly and return at the end of the holiday. On a Friday we sang hymns around the piano. 'When he cometh' and 'The morning bright with rosy light' were favourites. There were no hymn-books until Primary 3. The Missie, who was old (in her late fifties or early sixties?) wore a large nylon smock to protect her tweed skirt, twin-set and pearls from her grubby charges. School could not begin until the bus came out from Forfar, not usually a problem but it was sometimes delayed. On a few occasions she brought her small dog with her and it slept in a corner of the classroom. There were around forty pupils in the school at this time with approximately sixteen in the first three classes. We learned to read with Dick and Dora and Nip the Dog. Word boxes were old tobacco tins again. What a treat to get a new box which was passed around, under the cover of our opened desks, so we could all have a sniff! In the wee room discipline was by a slap on the knuckles. This was rare but swiftly executed when required!

Once in the 'big' room life was tougher. A new pupil wore a beautiful red cord velvet dress which she let me touch. As I admired it, my father hurled the wooden blackboard duster at me! His desk was a high pedestal with a stool behind it. Our desks had sloping lids, not very convenient for the new 'learning by discovery' being introduced. When I reached Primary 4 the new education act was being implemented. I didn't get my longed for ink pen, but a fat yellow biro. Cursive writing was out. I did however get away from learning tables and spelling tests to work on interactive cards involving experiments and problem solving. This extended to being ushered out of school to see a helicopter flying over, or to witnessing and then recording in our diaries a fall of snow in June. The visiting music teacher was an unpopular part of the school week. There were no budding opera singers in Kingsmuir at that time! PE involved a hike of 200 yards up the road to use the village hall for 'Music and Movement' being broadcast on the radio. An annual event was the rosehip collection. 'Real' money was paid to pupils brave enough to pick large quantities of rosehips. For lesser amounts a metal badge was awarded and for pupils like myself who didn't like prickles, and went after everyone else had had first pick, a little badge was given in exchange for a few hips.

School outings were invariably to Letham. I remember going to a 'real' play in the village hall, ' Rumplestiltskin', and sitting enthralled by the story. We also went to Letham for church services. I think buses were hired for these trips. We went on whole school trips to Edinburgh Zoo and I think once on a train journey. From

Primary 4 the 'big ones' got to go Youth Hostelling to Glen Doll, from where we climbed Dreish, Mayor, Corrie Fee, Jock's Road etc. under my father's supervision and to Forfar for a weekly swimming lesson, travelling on the service bus.

In the playground was a shelter called the 'soup kitchens' and a tarmac area, both level, and a fairly steep hill. Mainly we played running games, motor bikes for boys and horses for girls. There was no school garden. There was a wooden garage in the playground but this blew down during the hurricane which visited Kingsmuir (in ?1996) and landed on my father's car!

School meals were served in Kingsmuir Hall. We had to file in two's up 'The Loanie'. The meals were delivered from Forfar and were served by a local woman whose adage was 'a droppie dirt never hurt a pig'!

My days at Kingsmuir were secure and comfortable. My world was turned upside down when the upper school was closed and I had to attend a large Forfar Primary. I continued however to benefit from my father's sphere of influence. On the bus home after school I was being tormented by secondary pupils from a different village when a voice from the back of the bus called, 'Let her aff! She's the dominie's daughter.' My school bag was hastily restored to me and I had free passage to leave the bus!

Mr Ian Mathieson came from a private school in Edinburgh to be head teacher at Stracathro School in 1965:

The change from Edinburgh to an Angus farming community was a bit of a culture shock. The school was still heated by pot-bellied stoves. On my first day in the school I asked Bryan how he had spent the holidays. 'Ah muckt oot fower coorts', he replied. A visit by the school to the beautiful, formal gardens at Edzell Castle provoked a pupil into declaring that his faither wad hae a' that in tatties. After his very first day at school, Gavin's father asked how the day had gone. 'I gaed up the wrang dreel' was the reply. Later his father was chasing a cow that had broken loose when he flagged down my wife in the car and told her, 'Get efter that coo!'

Rosie and Dosie were two Muslim sisters who arrived one day from Yorkshire. At the family service school lunch they asked if they should eat what they thought might be pork, only to be told by the 'mother' that it wasn't pork it was Spam! They seemed to enjoy it and there were no repercussions from the parents.

Daniel arrived in mid-term from a very deprived area in the west of Scotland. He was nine but could not read. As usual with a new pupil I thought I should get to know him with a few questions.

> *Dominie: "What's your favourite colour, Daniel?"*
> *Daniel: "Glasgow Rangers." (Well I could figure that one out!)*
> *Dominie: "What's your favourite food, Daniel?"*

Daniel: "Chinky." (Ah, what happened to political correctness?)
Dominie: "What's your favourite subject at school, Daniel?"
Daniel: "Fightin'."
A Dominie's life was never boring!

Mrs Margaret Budge was Head Teacher at Logie Pert from 1965–1975:

While I was at Logie Pert the roll fluctuated between 11 and 18 pupils. I loved my time there and became very involved with the children's families. The parents became my friends. It suited me to live in the schoolhouse next door, as my own children were at the school, and if there was illness in our family I was nearby. On one occasion my son broke his leg in a playground accident. Fortunately the dinner van arrived and the patient and his older sister were dispatched to Stracathro Hospital while I had to stay with the pupils as there was no other adult in the building. I remember our dog had pups in the school house just at the time an Inspector decided to visit. However he said, "Just go through and see to them. I'll look after the children."

I was not always on my own but was sometimes joined by visiting teachers of music or art. We also used radio programmes for music etc. and commercial tapes to teach French. We were able to go on outings by bus or train to places like Anstruther. Parents joined us on these outings. In fact one mother was heard to say, "There's ower much money spent on equipment and no enough on trips."

Children from rural schools may find it difficult to move from a small primary to a large secondary school so we organised joint activities when we could. We had joint sports days with Craigo School and when our senior pupils went swimming they went on the bus unaccompanied to the pool and were able to meet children from other schools there.

Our education was not always in the classroom. Ian Grant, a parent of one of our pupils and a farmer, came to the school door one day to tell me, "Margaret, there are flamingos in Dun's Dish!" We all got into his landrover and rushed to see them. Another stormy April day a child arrived with a wee bird he had found. It had no feathers and was obviously very young. We went out and looked along the road for parent birds but could not find them. Someone came in with an old cage and we fed the bird from our fingers on chopped up worms and bits of mince. The children had to wear their painting shirts all day because the bird, a starling we called Rosie, flew around and landed on their shoulders. In June we decided to let it go. For a few days it came when I called. Then one day it didn't return.

I felt that one of the big advantages of the small rural school was that children could progress at their own pace without being so aware of the stage of each pupil as is the case in a bigger school.

62 *Logie Pert playground. Senior children painted the world map*

A story from Hillside School about the dentist's visit:

The caravan in which dental work was carried out was parked in the school playground. The headmaster sent a boy to find out if the dentist was ready to receive patients. "Knock on the door," he instructed. The boy returned a few minutes later to say, "Please Sir, I knocked on the door but they're no up yet!"

Mrs Aileen Beedie was for several years a school dentist in Angus and visited many rural schools:

We drew the short straw with the dental caravan and always visited the rural schools in the winter months. The smallest schools could only accommodate the smaller of the two caravans, a fairly elderly model. It had to be attached to an electrical output and a water outlet, a very cold business. The schools' water taps were not uniform, and we spent many frustrating hours trying to attach our hose so it would stay attached. So one memory is of frequently losing our water supply, which was happily pouring over the playground. Frozen hoses were a common occurrence and we had various ways of de-icing them! Our metallic dental instruments were also icy cold

91

each morning, in spite of leaving heating on in the van every night. On more than one occasion, at Dun School, we had to abandon our car, don our wellies, and plod up the hill through the snow until we reached the school.

We always had our coffee with the teacher at the school, and once there was tablet being made for a fund-raising sale. So we were roped in to stir the tablet! A sign of the times happened at a one-teacher school, where the said teacher was male. A wee five-year-old girl had had a very messy 'accident' in the toilet and of course the teacher was unable to clean her up for fear of potential accusations. So in mid January, in a very cold toilet, I found myself cleaning the wee soul up, and comforting her in her distress.

Children will be children, and at a school with the larger caravan, a double-axle job, we came in one morning to discover the two tyres on one side as flat as pancakes! What fun! We never did find out who did it. Later on we acquired a state of the art dental van – a truck with conversion. It had its own water tank and generator, so we were self-contained. The only problem was that I had to drive it into the school playgrounds. And it was much bigger than a car! A lasting memory is of sitting in the cab with Pauline, my assistant, both in our white jackets, and driving through Montrose with Pauline saying, "Everyone's looking at us ...."

Mrs Winnie MacDonald became Head Teacher at Farnell School in 1983:

I came from a big primary school in Gourock to Farnell and took over from Mr McNicol, the dominie. At first I found it difficult to understand the Doric tongue which many of the families used. One mother told me, "The loon's no comin' to school the day" to indicate his absence. I was keen to match parents to pupils so I asked one father at a local whist drive, "Who are you?" "I'm fine thanks," he replied, "How's yoursel'?"

It was compulsory at that time to live in the school house which was on the Laird's ground over the burn from the school. It had been the butler's house. The Laird was the Earl of Southesk who took a great interest in the children of the school. On one occasion he brought a huge wasp's bike to show the pupils.

When I started teaching in Farnell there were about 56 pupils in two school rooms. An assistant teacher took Primary 1, 2 and 3, and I took 4, 5, 6, and 7. The classes were in a separate building from the old school in which we had our dining room and gym hall. A visiting gym teacher came to school as well as an art teacher and a peripatetic music teacher. We had percussion instruments and recorders and had some wonderful concerts in the village hall and services in the Farnell church. The community supported everything we did. Visitors to the school included the dentist, the school nurse, the instrumental music teacher, and the travelling library.

63 *Farnell School, showing the classrooms (ringed) which were demolished at a later date. The area is now a car park*

Many of the children came from the castle holdings and from surrounding farms such as Fithie and Haughs of Kinnaird. They walked or cycled to school even in bad weather. I do remember one occasion when heavy snow and freezing conditions caused all the pipes to burst. A pupil was first to notice this. "Please miss", he said. "The burn's comin' in the dinner hall". The school had to be closed for a fortnight until a temporary pipe was laid across the bridge. Dung was spread over it to keep it from freezing again.

When I arrived in Farnell I had to order new desks as well as lots of new books and introduce workbooks for the children. The older pupils helped younger ones. I had to be very well prepared with work for seniors when I was teaching younger ones and vice versa. However I do think the children had a great education. We were able to go to Brechin High swimming pool. At first only Primary 6 and 7 were allowed but I managed to get them to take the whole school. We organised football matches against Edzell school. The whole village would turn out to cheer our team on the field beside the school which the Earl had given us. When it was time for Sports Day again it was a real community occasion. The Earl called it the Farnell Highland Games.

The highlight of the school year was the Christmas party. There were mince pies and carols at the school house. The children brought their party clothes and changed at lunch time. The children were very appreciative of what we did for them but were quite reticent about expressing this. One wee boy bringing a bunch of flowers would only say, "There's something for you in my saddlebag." Some weren't so impressed. One lad told his mother, "The new missus isn't very good at the piano. She has to use two hands."

When I came to Farnell in 1973 there were 72 rural schools. We had our own conferences and the Director of Education called us "The salt of the earth"!

64 *Early days in Farnell. This photograph was given by Celia Gray whose mother is the third child from the left in the front row*

Mary Faulkner, who was Head Teacher at Arbirlot School from 1992 until 1997, feels that the rural school had many advantages for some children:

There were 28 children at Arbirlot divided between two teachers. I taught Primaries 4 to 7. The pupils came from the village, surrounding farms and further afield. Some parents drove children out from Arbroath because they wanted a small school or because their child had had difficulty in a bigger school. On one occasion when a Primary 1 child came in from a nearby farm his three-year-old brother came too. His mother had to come to take him home. Younger children could be helped by working with older pupils and their learning was advanced by easier access to materials. Children were responsible for their own learning.

The children in my class had a rota for answering the telephone and giving the caller an appointment to meet or contact the head teacher at dinner time or play time, thus giving them a lot more responsibility than in larger schools. Another advantage of the small rural school is record keeping. The teacher knows and teaches a child for thee years, whereas sometimes in big schools, when records are passed on, things are missed.

Visiting teachers taught Art and Physical Education and all the children who wished could take advantage of violin lessons. All children from Primary 3 to Primary 7 got a chance to be in football and netball teams. Some local ladies came in and helped to teach country dancing, the children being able to go to Perth to dance. Farmers visited school to talk to children on, for example, the potato business. Children also visited the farms. The local minister came on a weekly basis to school, also coming to all special events. The pupils went to Church for services at other times. One farmer leased a piece of ground to the school. Parents of the children cleared the land and sowed grass for a play area.

We often went for nature walks in lunch time along the River Elliot. A lady from Arbirlot explained what to look for, names of wild flowers and so on. Other outings included a school trip to Dalguise where we stayed in an old house which Beatrix Potter supposedly had visited. Two other rural schools joined us on a visit to York.

The school was very important to the parents. In November each year a large fund-raising event was held. On one year £500 was collected. There was very much a family atmosphere in school. Even sports day was a real family event. It was held in the grounds of a large house and took the form of potted sports with mixed age teams.

The pupils cared for each other and many still kept in touch with me after they had gone to secondary school. The transition from such a small school to a large secondary was made easier by the socialisation with other rural schools whose pupils would be moving to the same secondary and good liaison between primary and secondary.

65 *The new intake at Kilry School in 2002 helped to ensure the viability of the school*

Anne Gibb was Head Teacher at Kilry Primary School for more than 20 years:

The school was a major part of my life from 1982 when I was asked to go to Kilry as a supply teacher. The following year I was appointed Head. The children's enthusiasm for learning made the work easier than it might have been,

There was a worrying period when Kilry Primary's viability was questioned. The support of the community to attract new blood reaped dividends in 2001 and 2002. The school roll now stands at 20. I hope Kilry School will continue to thrive in its lovely surroundings, supported by a strong community.

Angus Councillor Ruth Leslie Melville appreciated the difficulties facing Careston Primary School in 2004:

With no promise of an influx of pupils and difficulty in recruiting staff, parents are philosophical about the proposed closure. When Careston was closed recently for an update the pupils were very happy going to Tannadice and appreciated the facilities there. With transport provided I think the Careston parents would be happy with that alternative.

Education Director Jim Anderson commented on the factors influencing the possible closures of small rural schools such as Careston:

Careston School has a roll of 16 with no more than three pupils in any of the year groups. There are only two children in the area who will be of an age to enrol in Primary 1 in August. If a school is a one-teacher school then the effort required by whoever is appointed head teacher is significant. Last year the post of head teacher at Careston was advertised three times. It seems quite likely one of the reasons we failed to attract sufficient numbers for this post relates to a legitimate perception that the job is an immensely challenging one. The cost per pupil of maintaining Careston is £4774 against the Council average of £2480 and Scottish average of £2369. The estimated cost of bringing the school up to an improved but not necessarily ideal standard would be in excess of £250,000. In all the circumstances the recommended option is to formally consider the possible closure.

Careston School was officially closed at the end of June 2004.

The Best Years of Your Life?

Many of the people we interviewed remembered their schooldays with affection but for some it had not been a completely happy time. It would seem that the personality and dedication of the head teacher had a particularly important part to play in a small rural school as these comments show:

I attended my two-teacher primary school from 1966 to 1973. Classes 1 to 3 were in the 'wee room' divided by a sliding partition from the 'big room' which contained P4 to P7. I was too young to remember much about P1 to P3 teachers, but my mother tells me that I was very fond of the teachers I had during this period and what memories I have of that time are happy ones. Looking back on it, these teachers must have given the children a good grounding for the next four years of primary school life.

In P4 to P7 the day started with spelling a few words we had been told to learn and then we did the times tables by going round the class, doing them forwards and backwards. This was an ordeal for my friend who had a stammer, which always got worse during this. The Head would make him start again if he stammered and occasionally mimic him. To this day, despite being now a successful professional, this is still his abiding memory. Then we had to open our arithmetic books and carry on from wherever we had left off the previous day – at which point the Head would disappear to his house through an adjoining door. He would emerge later to say, "James, ring the bell!" to signal morning break.

The remainder of the morning would continue as the earlier part had, with occasional variations e.g. English/Grammar, Art (copy this picture), Craft (I made a couple of wicker baskets), or, on rare occasions, Music (a visiting music teacher would hand out chime bars and try to get us singing/ playing) The Head would not usually be in the room for any of this. Other lessons, which I only recall doing in the afternoon, were History (reading aloud extracts from a specific chapter, then copying it out) and Geography (same routine).

Occasionally we would listen to a nature programme on the radio. The Head would come in at the end, hand out paper and tell us to write about what we had just heard. He'd return later to collect these, and put them in a cupboard, never to be seen again. We had a small library and were given time to select a book to read.

There was always the threat of the 'belt', but I only saw it used twice. The Head however was so feared that, despite lengthy and frequent absences from the room, there was rarely a word spoken. On one occasion he crept back into the room while my friend and I were talking, and banged our heads together. Prizes were awarded and I was one of the lucky ones. I still have 'Harry the Dirty Dog' and a Ladybird book on reptiles and amphibians.

The annual school picnic was to Montrose, Arbroath or St Andrews. At Christmas the Head produced a film projector and showed short Disney films e.g. Donald Duck. We went swimming once a week and on occasion had football matches with another rural primary – a bit one-sided because they had so many older children than us, but we did have one famous victory! This was cancelled once because the Head found someone talking.

There was a shed at the top of the playground and a cloakroom/ kitchen where we were sometimes allowed to go in inclement weather. There were outside toilets. The boys played football constantly but now and again games like British Bulldog. School meals were delivered and heated up by our dinner-lady/cleaner.

With hindsight and knowledge of the education system, I now realise how appallingly I must have been educated between P4 and P7. I cannot recall actually being in a lesson where I was 'taught' as opposed to being set work to do (but I must have been). However, because of the emphasis on reading, writing and arithmetic, we were ahead of our peers when we went to secondary school.

Overall I was happy at primary school. I enjoyed reading and writing and there was no shortage of that. There was plenty of room to play football in the playground and I had good friends. The school gave stability and structure.

The Rural Schools Today

The rural schools today offer a breadth and variety of curriculum which would have amazed the teachers of earlier years. Even the smallest country school continues to provide a positive ethos. In visiting rural schools all over Angus we have been very aware of the high standard of education on offer and the quality of relationship with parents and the wider community.

A good example of the work of the small rural primary school can be found at Newtyle which in 2003 had four primary classes with 74 pupils in all. There is also a nursery class of 16 pupils. The head teacher, Rosina McNicoll explained to us how Newtyle, like other rural schools in Angus, endeavours to give children the experience of as wide a range of activities as possible.

Each year we take part in the Burns Festival where all children from P3–P7 learn a Scottish poem. This year P6/7 also took part in the Burns Art competition. Some children from P4–P7 entered the Angus Burns Singing Competition which is held in Forfar and they did extremely well. The Drama Club present a yearly show which is of a professional standard and much enjoyed by the whole community. This year's performance by P5–P7 pupils – An Ocean Odyssey – was a great success. The pupils in P4/5 took part in the Arbroath Festival this year. Although a very small class of 15 pupils, we received a commendation. Our P3 pupils have undertaken a business enterprise this session, which involves making and selling a variety of cards. The money they receive will go towards buying games etc. for the classroom. This class also held a mock wedding as part of their Religious and Moral Education studies.

We always try to incorporate visits which fit in with our projects. This year our P3 class visited Pictavia as part of their project on Picts and our P4/5 class visited Ancrum Road School Victorian classroom to experience lessons in the Victorian style. We managed to find a wonderful teacher to act the part of a Victorian teacher and she gave the children lessons using ink pens and slates.

We support a variety of charities each year, this year raising money for Food Aid (Africa), Children in Need, Comic Relief and UNICEF.

There is a range of extra-curricular activities for children. The Drama Club (P5–7), Scottish Country Dancing (P4–7), Cross Country (P5–7), Football (P5–7) and we take P6/7 to Dalguise for an Adventure Weekend or to France for a Language Detective Course.

We very much focus on the environment and build respect for this and people around us. In all of this we are very grateful for the constant support of the parents and the community who help us in much appreciated ways throughout the year.

Our nursery has undertaken major work in their play area with the support of the community and other services. This has been a huge effort but the results are very worthwhile.

Mrs Janet Coyle, Head Teacher at Glenisla Primary School became involved in a project which gave her pupils an experience of the lives of children in Greece, Austria and Slovenia.

Some time ago I attended a seminar in Oslo. The theme was 'It takes a village to raise a child' and it introduced me to the three year Comenious Project. Comenious was a Czech educationist who wanted to share best practice across Europe. Our school was linked with three others, one from Greece, one from Austria and one from Slovenia. During the first year the subject was singing and music and each school made CDs and /or cassettes in their own language and sent them to the partner schools to be learned. The photograph shows the culmination of the first year when teachers from the four schools met in Glenisla in September 2002. It was a wonderful international meeting in a small rural school. We held a ceilidh and sang the learned songs to each other. Then the Scottish children performed three dances; Haymakers' Jig, Flying Scotsman and Circassian Circle. We videoed the dancing so that the other schools could learn them for the second year of the project which was about dance and drama. The Glenisla children have recorded two stories and sent them to the partners. These were 'Collie Cam' and 'Davy the Hero'. During the years of the project the songs and dances and drama were not treated as extras but as part of the curriculum.

In may 2003 a Rural Schools Science Fair took place at Carmyllie Primary School. Pupils from Carmyllie, Collieston and Arbirlot were there. Angus Council, the Ranger Service, Montrose Basin Wildlife Centre staff, Dundee Botanic Gardens staff and other groups were represented.

Carmyllie PS head Victoria Keith said,

The children were all mixed up in inter-school groups according to their ages and stages, and had to carry out activities throughout the day. It was excellent and I would like this at the school again.

A spokeswoman for Angus council commented,

The event was a celebration of good practice in Angus and gave staff the opportunity to share their knowledge and expertise with colleagues.

66 *Drama: The pantomime at Glamis was 'Snow White and the Twelve Dwarves' and at Rosemount they performed 'Puss in Boots' at Christmas*

67 *Music: Airlie Primary School pupils were successful in the recorder group at Perthshire Provincial Mod*

68 *Construction Fun: Monikie Primary School was involved in the K'Nex Engineers for Britain Challenge*

69 *Science: Lintrathan pupils are pictured with some items purchased with a £500 grant awarded as part of Science Year*

70 *Information Technology: A well-equipped classroom at Kilry showing computer*

71 *Religious and Moral Education: A mock wedding at Newtyle was part of religious and moral education studies*

72 *Healthy Eating: The tuck shop at Eassie Primary*

73 *Fund raising: At Colliston Primary the children raised £820 by forming a mile of coins for CHAS*

74 *International Visitors: Glenisla Primary entertained international visitors*

75 *Modern Languages*

76 *Parents try to bring in new families: At Lintrathan Primary the new school garden is one of the parents' projects*

77 *New buildings and extensions: The extension to the school at Inverkeilor*

78 *New faces: New pupils at Tannadice school*

I Like My New School!

The Inverkeilor Primary School new extension was officially opened in February 2004. It has many new features to fit it for the 21st century.

The existing building has been remodelled and the structure and fabric upgraded with a full new heating system, high standards of insulation and finishes to extend the life of the facility. Photovoltaic cells on southerly roof aspects will take advantage of a green energy source and recycling of grey water from roof areas through a holding tank for use in flushing toilets will reduce running costs and water consumption. This contributes to lower annual revenue costs and assists in meeting government targets for the reduction on CO_2 emissions. Windcatchers are incorporated and located at ridge points to avoid the need for mechanical ventilation systems. These operate by introducing fresh air to internal rooms through a central pipe that in turn creates a pressure to remove stale air through a secondary duct.

Grant funding was accessed to support the photovoltaic system to meet the electrical demands of the school. Any excess electrical power generated is supplied to the national grid with credits awarded. The school is fitted with a Building Management System to monitor and remotely control the use of energy in the building.

The children are enthusiastic about their new environment.

Nursery pupils:

I like the pram and flushing the toilet.

I think it is pretty and nice.

Primary 1:

It has got fancy lights.

Primary 2:

The playground is fun because it is better.

Primary 3:

I like the colours.

Primary 5:

You can put all of your things in the cloakrooms and the pigeon holes are good for putting your gym kit in.

There is new furniture in the spare classroom. We have never had sofas in school before.

There are more water fountains.

It is all in one building so we do not have to run to another class.

The solar panels save energy.

When the sun is shining in your eyes you just close the blinds.

You have loads of computers beside each other and if you get stuck on something you can ask someone beside you in the computer area.

Appendix 1: The stages in Teacher Training

JUNIOR STUDENT'S CERTIFICATE.

Dunfermline High School Training Centre.

THIS IS TO CERTIFY that *Thomasina Muir*

completed a *two* years' course of training as a JUNIOR STUDENT at this

Centre on *June 30th* 19*10*.

I. The following subjects were included in the approved curriculum, and the
RECORDS OF WORK for that period, kept in terms of ARTICLE 10 (*a*), and the
JUDGMENTS OF THE EXAMINERS APPOINTED BY THE SCOTCH EDUCATION DEPARTMENT,
show that satisfactory progress has been made therein :—

English.	Mathematics (including Arithmetic).	Needlework.
History.	Experimental Science.	Physical Exercises.
~~Latin.~~	Geography.	Music.
French.	Drawing.	
~~German.~~	~~Wood~~work.	

II. The STUDENT has followed an approved course of *250* hours of systematic
training in the ART OF TEACHING the PRIMARY SCHOOL SUBJECTS, and
proficiency therein is rated as *Very Good*.

[OVER.

(7788) Wt 3100-95 2000 12/09 M & G Ltd 179-B

Edinburgh Provincial Committee for the Training of Teachers.

GENERAL CERTIFICATE.

It is hereby certified *that* ___Thomasina Muir___
completed on the twenty-eighth of June 1912, *to the satisfaction of this Committee and of the Scotch Education Department, an approved course of training extending over* two *years, that* her *attendance was* highly satisfactory, *that* her *conduct was* exemplary, *and that* she *is entitled to receive, and hereby does receive, this General Certificate in terms of Article* 33 *of the Regulations for the Preliminary Education, &c., of Teachers.*

It is also certified *that the final marks obtained by* her *in each of the Principal Subjects of the Professional Course of Training were as follows :—*

SUBJECT.	Training College.	University	SUBJECT.	Training College.	University
1. HISTORY OF EDUCATIONAL SYSTEMS AND THEORIES	V.G.	—	4. SCHOOL AND PERSONAL HYGIENE, including Physical Exercises	V.G.	—
2. PRINCIPLES OF TEACHING, including (in their bearing upon Teaching)—			5. PRESENT DAY EDUCATIONAL PROBLEMS	V.G.	
PSYCHOLOGY	Ex.		6. ENGLISH	V.G.	—
ETHICS	Ex.		7. PHONETICS AND VOICE PRODUCTION	V.G.	
LOGIC			8.		
3. METHODS AND PRACTICE OF TEACHING	Ex.A.		9.		

It is further certified *that* ___ *is recognised by the Department as a* **Certificated Teacher**, *as from the 1st August* 1912, *in terms of Article* 38 *of the Regulations, and as qualified to give instruction in the Ordinary Subjects of the Primary School Curriculum, and also in the Subjects and for the purposes specified hereunder, viz. :—*

SUBJECT.	† Recognised for the Purposes of Article 37.	SUBJECT.	† Recognised for the Purposes of Article 39 (Supplementary Courses).
1. MUSIC	Ex. +	A.—RURAL COURSE	
2. DRAWING	V.G.		
3. PHYSICAL EXERCISES			
4. NEEDLEWORK		B.—INDUSTRIAL COURSE	
5. EDUCATIONAL HANDWORK (Lower Course)	V.G. +		
6. „ „ (Higher Course)			
7.		C.—DOMESTIC COURSE	

The following Marks were awarded for

RELIGIOUS INSTRUCTION ‡ V.G.

PIANOFORTE V.G.

* NOTE.—The degree of proficiency attained in any subject is indicated by the mark Ex. = Excellent, V.G. = Very Good, G. = Good, F.G. = Fairly Good, F. = Fair, O. = Unsatisfactory, entered against the subject.
† A Cross (X) indicates recognition.
‡ The mark has been determined by the relative Church Authorities.

Granted in name and by authority of the Edinburgh Provincial Committee,

_____ *Principal of the Training College.*

_____ *Director of Studies.*

SCOTCH

EDUCATION DEPARTMENT.

TEACHER'S CERTIFICATE.

THE LORDS OF THE COMMITTEE OF THE PRIVY COUNCIL ON
EDUCATION IN SCOTLAND

Hereby Certify That _____

Thomasina Muir,

having successfully completed ___ two ___ *years of training, and
having satisfied the requirements as to Probationary Service laid down
in the Department's Regulations, is recognised by the Scotch Education
Department as a CERTIFICATED TEACHER for the purposes
of the Scotch Code, as from the First day of August, 19 12, and is
further recognised for the purposes of Article 37 (b) of the Regulations
for the Preliminary Education, Training, and Certification of Teachers
for Various Grades of Schools, as qualified to give instruction in the
following subjects :—*

Music

Drawing.

{ *Educational Handwork:*

{ *(Lower Course)*

*Under the provisions of the Superannuation Scheme for
Teachers, this Certificate will expire on the* 12 th *day of
February,* 19 57 *, when the teacher attains the age of Sixty-
five years, or upon retirement at any earlier date in terms of Article 9
of the Scheme.*

*Edinburgh
Provincial*

¹2

This Teacher
is recognised as
a specially qualified
Teacher of Infants
BY ORDER OF THE SCOTCH EDUCATION DEPARTMENT

Vice-President.

Verified _____

Verified & Date 2 " "41

Auchterderran School Board

Town House.

Lochgelly 25th July   1912 .

Dear Miss Muir,

<u>Auchterderran School</u>.

I beg to intimate that you have been appointed Assistant Teacher in the above school. The salary begins at £70. and rises by annual increments of £5 to £90. You will require to pay your own contributions under the new Superannuation Scheme. You will enter on duty on Tuesday, 27th August, from which date the engagement will run, and it will terminate with one month's notice on either side. I shall be glad to have your acceptance of office on these terms.

Yours faithfully,

Robert Small
Clerk.

Miss Thomasina Muir,
Woodend,
Cardenden.

Appendix 2: Extract from the Scotch Code (1874.)

34.   In every School receiving Annual Grants, the Managers must provide out of the School Funds, besides Registers of Attendance (Article 17*h*),—

> (*a.*)   A Diary or Log-Book.
>
> (*b.*)   A Portfolio to contain Official Letters, which should be numbered in the order of their receipt.

35.   The Diary or Log-Book must be stoutly bound and contain not less than 500 ruled pages.

36.   The principal teacher must make, at least once a week, in the Log-Book, an entry which will specify ordinary progress, and other facts concerning the school or its teachers, such as the dates of withdrawals, commencements of duty, cautions, illness, &c., which may require to be referred to at a future time, or may otherwise deserve to be recorded.

37.   No reflections or opinions of a general character are to be entered in the Log-Book.

38.   No entry once made in the Log-Book may be removed or altered otherwise than by a subsequent entry.

39.   The summary of the inspector's report, and any remarks made upon it by the Department, when communicated to the Managers, must be copied *verbatim* into the Log-Book, with the names and standing (*certified teacher of the——class*, or *pupil-teacher of the——year*, or *assistant teacher*) of all teachers to be continued on, or added to, or withdrawn from the school staff according to the decision of the Department upon the Inspector's report. The correspondent of the Managers must sign this entry, which settles the school staff for the year.

40.   The Inspector will call for the Log-Book [*and Portfolio*] at every visit, and will report whether it [*they*] appears to have been properly kept. He will specially refer to the entry pursuant to Article 39, and he will require to see entries accounting for any subsequent change in the school staff. He will also note in the Log-Book every visit of surprise (Article 12), making an entry of such particulars as require the attention of the Managers.

Appendix 3: School Boards and Attendance Requirements

School attendances were marked twice every day, once in the morning and once in the afternoon.

The Education (Scotland) Act of 1872 and 1878 had the following requirements:

1.   No person can take into his employment any child who is under Ten years of age (except as stated under 3, below) or who, being of the age of Ten years and not more than Fourteen years, has not obtained a certificate from one of her Majesty's Inspectors of Schools declaring that said child has passed the Fifth Standard prescribed by Article 28 of Scotch Code of 1878.

2.   Partial exemption from attendance at School in the case of a child above Ten years of age can be obtained only when such child has passed the Third Standard prescribed by the same article of the above named Code.

3.   The School Board may, if thought fit, exempt from attendance at School any child above Eight years of age whose service may be required for the necessary operation of farm work in seed time and harvest time, provided that the exemption is not for a longer period than six weeks, altogether annually.

4.   Applications for exemption must, in every case, be made to the school Board through the Clerk.

5.   No child whose attendance at School during the School year has been under 250 can be presented for examination by her Majesty's Inspectors on the day of his Inspection.

Appendix 4: Six Standards set by the Scotch Education Department

The Scotch Education Department set six standards. Before a pupil could progress to the next standard he had to satisfy the visiting inspector.

	Standard I.	Standard II.	Standard III.	Standard IV.	Standard V.	Standard VI.
Reading.	Easy book (approved by the Inspector), not confined to words of one syllable.	Reading, *with comprehension, easy narrative,* the book to be brought by the Inspector. *The scholar to point out the nouns in the passage read.*	Improved reading of plain narrative, the book to be brought by the Inspector. *The scholar to show comprehension of the meaning of the sentences read, and to point out the nouns, adjectives, and verbs.*	Reading intelligently a passage from some history book in use in the school, with parts of speech and explanation of sentences.	Reading with expression a short passage of prose or of poetry from class book approved by the Inspector, with explanation, grammar, and elementary analysis of simple sentences.	Reading, with improved expression, explanation, and grammatical analysis of passages selected by the Inspector.
Writing.	A line from the same book, copied in large or half-text on slates or in copy-books.	(a) A short sentence from the same book, dictated slowly word by word. (b) Writing large or half-text; copybooks to be submitted.	(a) Five lines from the same book, dictated slowly by a few words at a time. (b) Fair small-hand, with capital letters, and figures, to be shown in copy-books.	(a) Ten lines dictated slowly from the same book. (b) Improved small-hand, to be shown in copy-books.	Writing from memory the substance of a short story or narrative read out twice by the Inspector; spelling, grammar, and handwriting to be considered.	A short letter on a subject to be prescribed by the Inspector. The form of composition, spelling, grammar, and handwriting to be considered.
Arithmetic.	Notation and numeration up to 1000. Simple addition and subtraction of numbers of not more than three figures.	Notation and numeration up to 10,000. The multiplication table to 5 times 12. Simple addition and subtraction of sums of ten figures.	Notation and numeration up to 1,000,000. Four simple rules. Money and time tables.	Compound rules (money and common weights and measures). Aliquot parts of a pound sterling.	Practice, bills of parcels, and simple proportion.	Compound proportion, vulgar and decimal fractions.
History and Geography.			*Outlines of the History of Scotland, from Robert the Bruce to the Union of the Crowns. General outline of the Geography of Scotland.*		*More detailed knowledge of the History of Scotland, from Robert the Bruce to the Union of the Kingdoms (1707), with special knowledge of any historical events connected with the district in which the school is situated. Geography of Scotland, with special knowledge of the county in which the school is situated, and map drawing of it.*	*Outlines of the History of Great Britain from the Union of the Crowns to the death of George III. Geography of Great Britain, Continental divisions of the world, and outline of map.*

Appendix 5: Rural Schools on the Library-Bus route in the 1950s

>   Former Junior Secondary school now only
      Primary

†   School now closed

Aberlemno
Airlie
† Aldbar
Arbirlot
† Arrat
† Auchmithie
Auchterhouse
Barry
† Braes of Coull
† Careston
Carmyllie East
† Carmyllie West, Greystone
> Carnoustie Junior Secondary
† Carroch
† Chapelton
† Clova
Colliston
Cortachy
† Craichie
† Craig
> Craigo Junior Secondary
† Denside of Glenogil
Dun
Eassie
> Edzell Junior Secondary
† Farnell
† Fern
Ferryden
† Folda
† Fowlis Easter
> Friockheim Junior Secondary
Glamis
Glenisla
† Glenogilvy
† Glenprosen
† Guthrie
† Hillside
Inverarity

> Inverkeilor Junior Secondary
† Kettins
Kilry
† Kingoldrum
† Kingsmuir
† Kinnell
† Kinnettles
† Kirkbuddo
† Kirkden
> Letham Junior Secondary
Lethnot
Liff
Lintrathen
† Little Brechin
† Logie Pert
† Lunan
† Lundie
† Maryton
Mattocks
† Menmuir
† Memus
> Monifieth Junior Secondary
Monikie
† Muirhead of Liff
> Murroes Junior Secondary
Newbigging
> Newtyle Junior Secondary
† Oathlaw
† Padanaram
Panbride
Pitkennedy
† Rescobie
† Roundyhill
† Ruthven
† St Vigeans
Stracathro
Tannadice
Tarfside
Tealing
† Waterside
† Westerton of Rossie

115

Glossary

Catechism: A book containing instruction by means of a series of questions and answers on the religious doctrine of the church.

Disruption of the Church of Scotland: After prolonged disputes, 474 ministers of the Church of Scotland, out of a total of about 1200, largely supported by their congregations, signed the Deed of Demission and formed the Free Church.

Dominie: Headmaster.

EIS: The Educational Institute of Scotland is a schoolteachers' organisation incorporated by Royal Warrant in 1851; became a trade union.

Forfarshire Militia: A force raised from the civilian population of Forfarshire (Angus) after 1797 in the expectation of French invasion; a kind of Home Guard.

General Assembly: The governing body of the Church of Scotland which consists of ministers and elders sent up by presbyteries. It meets annually in May. A Lord High Commissioner is appointed each year to represent the sovereign but does not have any voting rights.

Heritors: Owners of heritable property in a parish who from the 17th century until 1872 were responsible for maintaining a school in the parish.

Glebe: A portion of land which many parish ministers were allotted to supplement their income.

HMI: His/Her Majesty's Inspectors of schools.

Jacobites: Supporters of the House of Stuart and its claim to the throne after the deposition of James VII in 1689.

Jeelie Piece: Two slices of bread with jam in between.

Kirk Session: A court of the church made up of the ministers and elders of a congregation.

Normal Colleges: teacher training institutions founded in the 1830s by voluntary societies in Edinburgh and Glasgow which received a Government grant.

Old Statistical Account: A statistical account of Scotland, the work of Sir John Sinclair, compiled 1791–98 from information provided by parish ministers, giving a description of the country parish by parish.

Parish: An area with a church and a minister.

Precentor: A person appointed to lead the congregation in the singing during church services.

Presbytery: The Church Court next above the Kirk Session made up of the minister and one ruling elder from each congregation in an area.

Scotch Code: See Appendix 2.

Sessional Schools: Schools set up by Kirk Sessions which after 1833 received a modest Government grant.

Tawse: Leather strap used for punishment in schools by striking the palm of the hand.

Term Time: Farming seasons of employment at Candlemas (February), Whitsun (May), Lammas (August), Martinmas (November).

The Three Rs: Reading, writing and arithmetic.

Bibliography

Adams, David G *Usan or Fishtoun of Ullishaven*, Brechin, 1993

Anderson, R D *Education and Opportunity in Victorian Scotland*, OUP, 1983

Clark, M and P Munn (eds) *Education in Scotland: policy and practice from pre-school to secondary*, Routledge, London, 1997

Caughie, D (ed) *The Glasgow Infant School Magazine, First Series*, London, 1863

Cruickshank, Helen B *Voices from the Waterside*, Forfar, 1908

Currie, James *The Principles and Practice of Common School Education*, Thos Laurie, Edinburgh, 1870

Douglas, Andrew *History of the Village of Ferryden*, Montrose, 1855

Edwards, D H *Among the Fisherfolks of Usan and Ferryden*, Advertiser, Brechin, 1921

Fraser, Rev W Ruxton *St. Mary's of Old Montrose*, Blackwood and Sons, Edinburgh, 1896

Gray *Gray's Introduction to Arithmetic*, Edinburgh, 1866

Glamis Publishing Group *Glamis, A Village History*, 2000

Hendrie, Wm F *The Dominie*, John Donald, Edinburgh, 1997

Hill, Wentworth and Wood, H G *The Land of Poetry*, London, 1930

Hunter, S Leslie *The Scottish Educational System*, Oxford, 1971

Kidd, Ishbel and Gill, Peter *The Feuers of Letham*, ADC Libraries and Museums, 1989

Insh, George Pratt *School Life in Old Scotland*, EIS, Edinburgh, 1928

Inglis, W Mason *Annals of an Angus Parish*, Forfar, 1898

Jessop, J C *Education in Angus*, University of London Press, 1931

Jervise, Andrew *Memorials of Angus and Mearns*, Edinburgh, 1861

Jones, Emily G *Manual of Needlework and Cutting Out*, Longmans Green, London, 1889

Kinnettles Heritage Group *Kinnettles Kist*, 2000

Law, Annie *Carmyllie Parish Church, 1500–2000*, Private Press, 2001

Law, Anne *The Country School Diary*, Tillicoultry, 1985

Marshall, William *Historic Scenes in Forfarshire*, Edinburgh, 1875

Michie, M F *Studies in the History of Glenesk: Church and School, Book 5,* Glenesk Museum

Michie, M F *Glenesk: The History and Culture of an Angus Community*, compiled and edited by A Fenton and J Beech, Tuckwell Press, 2001

Morrison, D *School Log Books and other Sources*, Dundee College of Education, 1981

Morrison, D and Mouat, A *Montrose Old Church, A History*, Montrose Review Press, 1991

Morrison, D and Reynolds, I *Changed Days in Montrose*, Montrose Review Press, 1999

Murray J and Macmillan A *Scotland the Nation, Scottish History Series II*, Macmillan, 1932

Nairn, F C *A Scheme of Elementary Object Drawing for Day Schools*, Grant, Glasgow, 1909

Nelson *The Royal School History of Scotland*, Nelson, Edinburgh *1881*

Orr, Margaret *Educating the Glens Bairns*, Private Press

Reid, Alan *The Bards of Angus and the Mearns*, John Menzies, 1897

Scotland, J *The History of Scottish Education*, London, 1969

Smith, J W D *Introduction to Scripture Teaching*, Thos Nelson, 1949

Taylor, E *Why Friockheim*, Finavon Print, 2001

Towers, Allan *A Child's Aesop*, Hodder and Stoughton, 1902

Primary Sources

The Statistical Account of Scotland, 1791-1799, Vol. XIII, Angus, EP Publishing Ltd, 1976

The New Statistical Account of Scotland: Forfar and Kincardineshire (Second ed), Edinburgh, 1865

Third Statistical Account of Scotland, The County of Angus, Edinburgh 1977

Records of the Presbytery of Brechin (1729–38; 1791–94)

Session Records of Montrose Old Parish Church (1800–33)

Session Records of Montrose Old Parish Church (1834–73)

School Log-books for the County of Angus

Admission Records for Angus Schools

Angus School Board Records: Dun; Dunnichen; Eassie and Nevay; Fearn; Inverkeilor; Kirkbuddo; St Vigeans; Tannadice.

The Montrose Year Book and Directory 1893–95

Newspapers

The Montrose Review

The Kirriemuir Free Press

The Forfar Dispatch

The Arbroath Herald

The Brechin Advertiser

Index of Schools

Index of People

EBB and FLOW
Aspects of the History
of Montrose Basin

Montrose Basin Heritage Society

Published October 2004

ISBN 1 874012 45 8

250 x 176mm; xiv,142 pp; 56 b/w illustrations; pb £7·99

Montrose Basin Heritage Society was formed in 1999 to promote the study of the geological origins, the fauna and flora and man's influence during the passage of time of Montrose Basin.

An internationally important site, the Basin is already renowned for its wildlife, now ably promoted by the Scottish Wildlife Trust's Visitor Centre, at Rossie Braes. The purpose of this book is to shed some light on the people who have lived around its shores and exploited its resources and who have shaped or influenced the surrounding landscape. To this end, individual studies of several important aspects of the history of the area are presented – Prehistoric Archaeology; the Romans in Montrose; Place-names; Erskine of Dun and the Reformation; Langley Park and its Owners; Salmon Fishing and Mussel Cultivation. Additionally there is a chapter on the geology of the Basin explaining its creation over the course of 400 million years; also a comprehensive Time Line charting significant events in the area from the early geological periods through man's prehistoric ages and the more recent centuries of modern history up to the millennium.

One of the contributors has provided a number of line drawings and maps and the volume is profusely illustrated with other material from various sources, including some reproductions of the works of the acclaimed local artist William Lamb.

A LIFE ON THE LAND
FARMING IN ANGUS 1934–1994

Harry Brown
Edited by David Orr

Published June 2003

ISBN 1 874012 32 6
210 x 148mm; 76 pp; illustrations and map; pb £4·75

Harry Brown's working life on the land began in 1934 and lasted until his retirement, 60 years later, in 1994. Initially fee'd to work at farms around Forfar in Angus, usually for a term of six months, he progressed through the bothy system from 'loon' to 'first horseman', eventually ending up managing his own farm. During his time Harry witnessed many changes in agricultural practices and these are all documented in his fascinating account. Memories of working with horses, the feeing markets and bothy life are shared along with glimpses of some of his many fellow workers.

Possessing an uncanny ability to clearly recall people and events from his past, Harry's reminiscences had not been written down until about three years ago when he related them to David Orr, who edited them for publication.

Anyone interested in the countryside and history of Angus will appreciate the authentic voice of the author in this welcome addition to the agricultural and social history of twentieth-century Scotland – subjects more usually the preserve of specialist writers and academic researchers.

Sadly Harry Brown died in May 2004, but not before he had witnessed the tremendous interest aroused by his book of memoirs.

The Pinkfoot Press

Balgavies, Forfar, Angus DD8 2TH

inbox@pinkfootpress.co.uk